Weaving It Together

Connecting Reading and Writing

THIRD EDITION

2

Milada Broukal

HEINLE
CENGAGE Learning™

Australia • Brazil • Japan • Korea • Mexico • Singapore • Spain • United Kingdom • United States

HEINLE
CENGAGE Learning™

Weaving It Together 2: Connecting Reading and Writing, Third Edition
Milada Broukal

Publisher: Sherrise Roehr

Acquisitions Editor: Tom Jefferies

Development Editor: Catherine Black

Director of Global Marketing: Ian Martin

Director of US Marketing: Jim McDonough

Senior Product Marketing Manager:
Katie Kelley

Marketing Manager: Caitlin Driscoll

Marketing Assistant: Anders Bylund

**Director of Content and Media
Production:** Michael Burggren

Content Project Manager: Mark Rzeszutek

Print Buyer: Susan Spencer

Cover Design: Page2 LLC

Compositor: Glyph International

Photo Research: Terri Wright Design,
www.terriwright.com

For product information and technology assistance, contact us at
Cengage Learning Customer & Sales Support, 1-800-354-9706

For permission to use material from this text or product,
submit all requests online at **cengage.com/permissions**
Further permissions questions can be emailed to
permissionrequest@cengage.com

Library of Congress Control Number: 2009939627

ISBN-13: 978-1-4240-5741-2

ISBN-10: 1-4240-5741-8

Heinle
20 Channel Center Street
Boston, MA 02210
USA

Cengage Learning is a leading provider of customized learning solutions with office locations around the globe, including Singapore, the United Kingdom, Australia, Mexico, Brazil, and Japan. Locate your local office at:
international.cengage.com/region

Visit Heinle online at **elt.heinle.com**

Visit our corporate website at **www.cengage.com**

Text Credits: p. 181: "This Is Just to Say" by William Carlos Williams, from THE COLLECTED POEMS: VOLUME I copyright 1938 by New Directions Publishing Corp. Reprinted by permission of New Directions Publishing Corp.

Printed in the United States of America
2 3 4 5 6 7 11 10

Brief Contents

Contents

A Message from the Author

Approach

Weaving It Together, Book 2, is the second in a four-book series that integrates reading and writing skills for students of English as a second or foreign language. The complete program includes the following books: Book 1–Beginning Level; Book 2–High Beginning Level; Book 3–Intermediate Level; and Book 4–High Intermediate Level.

The central premise of **Weaving It Together** is that reading and writing are interwoven and inextricable skills. Good readers write well; good writers read well. With this premise in mind, **Weaving It Together** has been developed to meet these objectives:

1. To combine reading and writing through a comprehensive, systematic, and engaging process designed to integrate the two effectively.
2. To provide academically bound students with serious and engaging multicultural content.
3. To promote individualized and cooperative learning within moderate- to large-sized classes.

Through its systematic approach to integrating reading and writing, **Weaving It Together** teaches ESL and EFL students to understand the kinds of interconnections that they need to make between reading and writing in order to achieve academic success.

Organization of the Text

Weaving It Together, Book 2 contains eight thematically organized units, each consisting of two interrelated chapters. Each unit begins with a set of questions to engage the student into the theme of the unit. Each chapter begins with a reading, moves on to a set of activities designed to develop critical reading skills, and culminates with a series of interactive writing exercises.

Each chapter contains the same sequence of activities:

1. **Pre-Reading and Predicting Activities:** Each chapter opens with a photograph, a set of discussion questions, and a vocabulary matching exercise. The pre-reading activity prepares students for the reading by activating their background knowledge and encouraging them to call on and share their experiences. The key vocabulary exercise acquaints them with the words that appear in the reading.
2. **Reading:** Each reading is a high-interest passage related to the theme of the unit. Selected topics include delicacies, killer bees, and biotechnology. The final unit contains readings from literature.

3. **Vocabulary:** Three types of vocabulary exercises practice the vocabulary contained in the reading. "Vocabulary in Context" uses the new words in the context in which they were used in the reading. "Vocabulary Building" and "Vocabulary in New Context" help students extend their vocabulary skills to new contexts by, for example, learning to recognize collocations, synonyms, or antonyms. Additionally, once per unit a "Word Partnership" box provides a complete collocation of a vocabulary word taught in that chapter. These are included to expand students' knowledge of how words go together in order to improve reading fluency.

4. **Reading Comprehension:** There are two types of reading comprehension exercises to check students' reading comprehension: "Looking for the Main Ideas" concentrates on a general understanding of the reading; and "Looking for Details" focuses on developing skimming and scanning skills.

5. **Discussion Questions:** Students work in small or large groups to discuss questions that arise from the reading. The discussion questions ask students to relate their experiences to what they have learned from the reading.

6. **Critical Thinking Questions:** These questions are much more challenging than the discussion questions. When students think critically about a given topic, they have to consider their own relationship to it, and thus the interaction with the topic is greater. Students are encouraged to interact in small or large groups to discuss or debate these questions, giving the classroom a more meaningful environment.

7. **Writing Skills:** In connection with each of the 16 readings, a different aspect of writing at the paragraph level is presented. These aspects include writing topic and supporting sentences, capitalization and punctuation, and using transitions. Exercises on the points taught provide reinforcement.

8. **Writing Practice:** Students are asked to write a paragraph, using the ideas they have generated in the discussion section and the grammar points they have practiced. The text takes them through the writing process one step at a time. First they write sentences about themselves in answer to questions presented in the text. Then they develop an outline in the form of a paragraph, using a checklist (on their own or with a partner) to check their paragraphs and then making any necessary alterations. Teachers are encouraged to add to the checklist any further points they consider important. In the fifth step, students are encouraged to work with a partner or their teacher to correct spelling, punctuation, vocabulary, and grammar. Finally, students prepare the final version of their paragraphs.

Weaving It Together: Optional Expansion and Review Activities

The final page of each unit, entitled "Weaving It Together," offers three types of expansion and review activities:

1. **Timed Writing:** To prepare them for exam writing, students are given a 50-minute timeframe to write paragraphs similar to the "Writing Practice" they have worked on in the unit. Teachers may change the 50-minute timeframe to one that suits their requirements.

2. **Connecting to the Internet:** These activities give students the opportunity to develop their Internet research skills. This activity may be done in a classroom setting, under the teacher's guidance, or—if students have Internet access—as a homework task leading to a classroom presentation or discussion.

3. **What Do You Think Now?:** Students are asked to review their answers from the "What Do You Think?" questions at the start of each unit. The questions review the information they learned while completing the unit.

Journal Writing

In addition to having students do projects and exercises in the book, I strongly recommend that you instruct them to keep a journal in which they correspond with you. It gives them an opportunity to tell you what they like, what they dislike, what they understand, and what they don't understand. By having students explain what they have learned in the class, you can discover whether they understand the concepts taught. In its finest form, journal writing becomes an active dialogue between teacher and student that permits you to learn more about your students' lives and to individualize their language instruction.

Note for the New Edition

In this new edition of **Weaving It Together**, **Book 2**, I have added a quiz at the beginning of each chapter to engage students in the theme of the chapter. The quiz is repeated at the end of the chapter so that students can check how much information they have learned from the chapter. In addition to the discussion questions, critical thinking questions have been added to give students the opportunity to develop their thinking skills. For those who need to write under constrictions of time, a timed writing activity has been included at the end of each chapter. I have also expanded the Internet activities. I hope that you will enjoy using these new features and that **Weaving It Together** will continue to help you toward success.

Your
Personality

What Do You Think?

Answer the questions with your best guess. Circle **Yes** or **No**.

Do you think . . .

1. fifteen percent of the population is left-handed?   **Yes**   **No**
2. intelligent people have heavier brains?   **Yes**   **No**
3. right-handed people are generally good at math and are
   practical and safe?   **Yes**   **No**
4. the Chinese believe there are four basic shapes of the face?   **Yes**   **No**
5. the Chinese believe the diamond shape is one of the shapes
   of the face?   **Yes**   **No**

Chapter 1

Right Brain,
Left Brain

Pre-Reading

Discuss the answers to these questions with your classmates.

1. Do you know the names of the people in the pictures on page 1?
2. For what are they famous?
3. All of them are the same in one way. What do you think it is?

Key Vocabulary

Do you know these words? Match the words or phrases with the meanings.

1. in common ___c___
2. population ___d___
3. logic ___f___
4. have things in order ___b___
5. punctual ___g___
6. recognize ___e___
7. exceptions ___h___
8. message ___a___

a. instruction or news sent to someone or something
b. have things in their right place
c. the same
d. number of people who live in a place
e. remember having heard or seen before
f. thinking that follows rules
g. on time; not late
h. people or things that do not belong with the others

Reading

Right Brain, Left Brain

Track 1

1   **W**hat do Leonardo da Vinci, Paul McCartney, and Julia Roberts have **in common**? They are all left-handed. Today about 15 percent of the **population** is left-handed. But why are people left-handed? The answer may be in the way the brain works.

5   Our brain is like a **message** center. Each second, the brain receives more than a million messages from our body and knows what to do with them. People think that the weight of the brain tells how intelligent you are, but this isn't true. Albert Einstein's brain weighed 1,375 grams, but less intelligent people may have heavier brains. What is important is the quality of the

10 brain. The brain has two halves—the right brain and the left brain. Each half is about the same size. The right half controls the left side of the body, and the left half controls the right side of the body. One half is usually stronger than the other. One half of the brain becomes stronger when you are a child and usually stays the stronger half for the rest of your life.

15   The left side of the brain controls the right side of the body, so when the left brain is stronger, the right hand will be strong and the person may be right-handed. The left half controls speaking, so a person with a strong left brain may become a good speaker, professor, lawyer, or salesperson. A person with a strong left brain may have a strong idea of time and will probably be

20 **punctual**. The person may be strong in math and **logic** and may like to **have things in order**. He or she may remember people's names and like to plan things ahead. He or she may be practical and safe. If something happens to the left side of the brain, the person may have problems speaking and may not know what day it is. The right side of his or her body will become weak.

25   When the right side of the brain is stronger, the person will have a strong left hand and may be left-handed. The person may prefer art, music, and literature. The person may become an artist, a writer, an inventor, a film director, or a photographer. The person may **recognize** faces, but not remember names. The person may not love numbers or business. The person

30 may like to use his or her feelings, and not look at logic and what is practical.

If there is an accident to the right side of the brain, the person may not know where he or she is and may not be able to do simple hand movements.

35   This does not mean that all artists are left-handed and all accountants are right-handed. There are many **exceptions**. Some right-handers have a strong right brain, and some left-handers have a strong left brain. The best thing would be to use both right and left sides of the brain. There are people who learn to do two things at the same time. They can answer practical questions on the telephone (which uses the left brain) and at the same time play the piano (which uses the right brain), but this is not easy to do!

Vocabulary

A. Vocabulary in Context

Complete the sentences with the following words.

8 exceptions	4 logic	7 punctual
5 have things in order	3 message	6 recognize
1 in common	2 population	

1. Leonardo da Vinci and Julia Roberts have something _____. They are both left-handed.
2. About 15 percent of the _____ is left-handed.
3. Each part of our body sends a _____ to the brain.
4. Right-handed people may not do something because they feel like it. They may do it because there is _____ to it.
5. A right-handed person may like to be neat and _____.
6. A left-handed person may look at a face and _____ the person.
7. A right-handed person doesn't like to be late. He or she is _____.
8. We cannot say that all right-handers have strong left brains and all left-handers have strong right brains. There are _____.

Word Partnership	Use **message** with:
v.	give *someone* a message, **leave** a message, **read** a message, **take** a message, **deliver** a message, **get** a message, **hear** a message, **get** a message **across**, **spread** a message
adj.	clear message, **important** message, **urgent** message, **powerful** message, **simple** message, **strong** message, **wrong** message

B. Vocabulary in New Context

Answer the questions with complete sentences.

1. What do you and your classmates have in common?

   We are all right-handed

2. Do you like to have things in order? Give an example.

   I like to place my books on the shelf neatly

3. Do you know someone who is always punctual?

   My mother is always punctual

4. What is the population of your country?

   The population of my country is

5. How do you recognize a person from a distance?

   I recognize a person by appearance, clothes and manners.

6. How do you usually leave a message for someone?

   I usually leave a message by calling, sending an email or texting

7. What is an exception to a rule in English grammar or spelling?

   Have, go, do are the exceptions in English grammar

C. Vocabulary Building

hw

Complete these sentences with the words from the box.

| **to weigh** (*verb*) | **weight** (*noun*) | **weighty** (*adj.*) |

1. After the accident to the left side of his head, his memory became a
   ___weighty___ problem.
2. He is very logical and likes ___to weigh___ the good and bad sides of each step he takes.

| **to populate** (*verb*) | **population** (*noun*) | **populous** (*adj.*) |

3. Mexico City is the most ___populous___ city in North America.
4. What is the ___population___ of New York City?

remember

| **to recognize** (*verb*) | **recognition** (*noun*) | **recognizable** (*adj.*) |

5. He can always ___recognize___ a face, but he has difficulty remembering names.
6. She walked by me and showed no sign of ___recognition___.

Reading Comprehension

A. Looking for the Main Ideas

Read the passage again, and look for the **main ideas**. Circle the letter of the best answer.

1. People are right-handed or left-handed because of _____.
   a. the population
   (b.) the way the brain works
   c. Paul McCartney and Julia Roberts
   d. the messages the brain receives

2. The brain _____.
   (a.) has two halves
   b. has two left halves
   c. is heavier in intelligent people
   d. is lighter in intelligent people

3. Each side of the brain _____.
   a. likes language and math
   b. controls the same things
   (c.) controls different things
   d. changes all the time

B. Looking for Details

Read the passage again, and look for **details**. Circle **T** if the sentence is true. Circle **F** if the sentence is false.

1. Fifty percent of the population is left-handed.   T   **F**
2. The weight of the brain does not tell how intelligent you are.   **T**   F
3. A right-handed person may prefer music and art.   T   **F**
4. A person with a strong right brain may be good at recognizing faces.   **T**   F
5. Some people can use both sides of the brain at the same time.   **T**   F
6. A person with a strong right brain may not be practical.   **T**   F

Discussion Questions

Discuss the answers to these questions with your classmates.

1. Do you think children should be forced to be right-handed?
2. Does the word *left* have a negative meaning in your language? Is it bad to be left-handed in your country?
3. Ask a left-handed person these questions:
   - Are your parents left-handed?
   - When you play tennis or other sports, do you use your left hand or your right hand?
   - When you were a child, did people try to make you right-handed?
   - Do you want to be right-handed?
   - What things do you find difficult to use (for example, scissors, can openers)?
   - Do you think you write slower than a right-handed person?

   In groups, discuss the answers you get.

Critical Thinking Questions

Discuss the answers to these questions with your classmates.

1. Which part of your brain do you think has the most influence on you, the right or left? Why do you think that? Which character traits do you wish you had that you don't have?
2. What good and bad character traits do people expect in logical (right-handed) people and artistic (left-handed) people? Are these ideas true? Do you think it's possible to be logical *and* artistic? Why or why not?

Writing

Writing Skills

A. Organizing: *The Paragraph Form*

In this book, you will learn how to write a good paragraph. Before you start to write, it is important for you to know the requirements of good paragraph form.

Instructions on Paragraph Form

1. Use lined paper or a new document in a word processing program on a computer.
2. Write your name, the date, and the course number in the upper right-hand corner of the page.
3. Write a title in the center at the top of the page. Capitalize the first word, last word, and all important words in the title. Do not capitalize *the*, *a*, *an*, or prepositions unless they begin the title.
4. Leave a 1-inch margin on both sides of the page. (Your teacher may ask you to leave a margin on the right-hand side also.) A word processing program will do this for you.
5. Indent the first line of every paragraph. When you write by hand, indent the first line about one inch from the margin. When you type, indent the first line five spaces. In business letters, you do not have to indent the first line of every paragraph.
6. Write on every other line of the paper, or use double-spaced lines if you are using a computer.
7. Capitalize the first word in each sentence, and end each sentence with a period.

Look at the example paragraph on page 9.

	Yumi Ono
○	March 3, 2011
	ESL 163

	Left-Handed People	*Center the title.*
Indent the first line.	Left-handed people have many problems living in a world for	
Capitalize the first word in each sentence.		
	right-handed people. First, driving a car may be a problem. All	
1-inch margin		
	the important things in the car are on the right. For example,	*1-inch margin*
	the ignition switch, the gear shift, the accelerator, and the	
○	brake are all on the right. Second, using a computer may be a	
	problem. Computers are again made for right-handed people,	
	and all the important keys are on the right. These include the	
	delete key, the enter key, the period, the comma, and other	
	important punctuation marks. In conclusion, left-handed people	
	have to work harder than right-handed people to do simple	
	things.	
○		

B. Punctuation and Capitalization

A sentence always begins with a capital letter and ends with a period (.), an exclamation point (!), or a question mark (?). The first word after a comma (,) begins with a small letter.

Capitalization Rules

Here are some rules for using capital letters.

1. Capitalize the first word in a sentence.

Today, about 15 percent of the population is left-handed.

2. Capitalize the pronoun *I*.

Paul and I are left-handed.

3. Capitalize all proper nouns. Here are some proper nouns:

a. Names of people and their titles:

John McEnroe	Mr. John Smith
Napoleon	Dr. Mary Roberts
Marilyn Monroe	

b. Names of places you can find on a map:

Verdugo Road	Times Square
Central Avenue	Canada
Lake Victoria	London, England

c. Names of nationalities, races, languages, and religions:

American	Hispanic
Asian	Muslim
Catholic	Arab

d. Names of specific organizations (schools, businesses):

University of California	Glendale College
Bank of America	Safeway
International Students Club	Red Cross

e. Names of school subjects with course numbers:

English 101	Spanish 01A

f. Names of days, months, and special days:

Monday	Independence Day
May	Halloween

g. Names of special buildings and bridges:

White House	Golden Gate Bridge

Exercises

1. Change the small letters to capital letters where necessary.

1. st. mary's college is located in boston, massachusetts.
2. in august 1959, hawaii became the fiftieth state of the united states.
3. I parked my car on the corner of greenwood avenue and lexington.
4. maria is a student from peru. she speaks spanish, french, and italian.

5. there are no classes during christmas, easter, and thanksgiving vacations.
6. students who are buddhist, muslim, christian, and jewish all got together to help.
7. I am taking three classes this semester: english 120, spanish 1A, and business administration.
8. have you been to see the white house in washington, d.c.?

2. Find the mistakes. There are 10 mistakes in grammar and capitalization. Find and correct them.

There are more than 500 million left-handed people in the world. There are also many left-handers who are famous. Recent american president who are left-handed are Ronald Reagan, bill Clinton, and Barack obama. Actors such as tom Cruise and robert De Niro and women like queen Elizabeth II and nicole Kidman is also left-handed. In the old days, people thought left-handed people were bad. In japan a long time ago, a man could ask for a divorce if he found that his wife was left-handed. Today, it's not bad to be left-handed.

3. Answer the following questions. Use capital letters where necessary.

1. What is your full name?

_____

2. Write the names of three other students in your class.

_____

_____

_____

3. What languages do you speak?

_____

4. Write the names of three other languages that students in your class speak.

_____

5. Where do you come from (city and country)?

_____

6. Write the names of five holidays that you know (in the United States or your country).

_____

_____

_____

7. Write the name and address of your school or college.

_____

_____

_____

_____

8. What classes are you going to take this year?

_____

_____

_____

C. How to Write a Title

A title tells the reader the topic of the paragraph. A title is usually a word or phrase. If it is a sentence, it should not be a long sentence.

Remember These Points

1. Capitalize the first word, last word, and all important words in the title. Do not capitalize prepositions and articles.

Exception: Capitalize an article that begins the title.

2. Do not underline or italicize the title.
3. Do not use a period (.), or a comma (,) at the end of the title. Do not use quotation marks unless it is the name of a poem or short story. You can use an exclamation mark (!) or a question mark (?) at the end of the title.

Examples of titles:

Stronger Right or Left Brain?

The Importance of Having a Friend

My First Day in the United States

Learning Can Be Fun, Too!

Exercise

4. Say what is wrong with the titles below. Then write the titles in the correct way.

1. Eating In The United States Of America.

Eating in the United States of America

2. "Learning english Is Important."

Learning English is Important

3. I have many problems because I am living away from my family.

Living away from Family Causes Problems

4. the Most Important Day Of My Life

The Most Important Day of My Life

Just For Fun: Do You Have a Stronger Left Brain or Right Brain?

This simple writing test will tell you which side of your brain is strongest.

1. Write your name on a piece of paper.
2. Did your pen point away from you when you wrote? Was your hand below the line of writing (straight writing)?
3. Did the pen point toward you? Was your hand above the line of writing (hooked writing)?

You have a stronger right brain if
　. . . you write straight with your left hand. (See picture 1.)
　. . . you write hooked with your right hand. (See picture 2.)

You have a stronger left brain if
　. . . you write straight with your right hand. (See picture 3.)
　. . . you write hooked with your left hand. (See picture 4.)

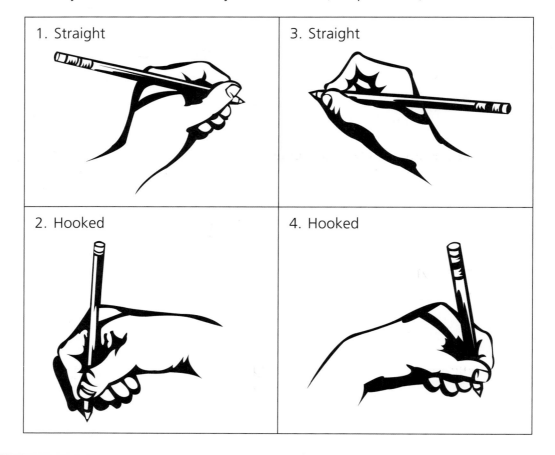

1. Straight　　　3. Straight

2. Hooked　　　4. Hooked

Chapter

Let's Face It

Pre-Reading

Discuss the answers to these questions with your classmates.

1. How are the faces of the two people in the photos similar?
2. What is the shape of their faces?
3. What different shapes do faces have?
4. Who do you most look like in your family?

Key Vocabulary

Do you know these words? Match the words with the meanings.

1. jaw ___g___
2. cheekbones ___f___
3. confident ___e___
4. will ___a___
5. creative ___d___
6. generous ___c___
7. fragile ___b___

a. strength of mind to control your actions
b. easily broken
c. willing to give
d. showing artistic ability
e. having a strong belief in your ability
f. the bones below and beside the eyes
g. the bony parts of the face that hold the teeth

Reading

 Let's Face It

Track 2

1   **S**ome people believe that the shape of a person's face shows the general character of the person. The Chinese believe that there are eight basic shapes of the face, and each shape shows a special character. The shapes are round, diamond, rectangle, square, triangle, narrow forehead and wide **jaw**, wide

5   forehead and square chin, and wide forehead and high **cheekbones**. Here is what people say about these shapes.

     Round faces have high and flat cheekbones, flat ears, wide noses, and strong mouths with thin lips. People with round faces are very intelligent, and they prefer to work with their brain instead of their body. People with round

10 faces are **confident** and usually live a long life.

     Many movie stars and famous women have diamond faces. The diamond face is narrow at the top and has a pointed chin. The Chinese believe that it is lucky if you meet a man or a woman with a diamond face before you go to an important meeting. People with this type of face are generally lucky in

15 love and in their jobs. They may not be happy when they are young, but they get what they want later in their lives. People with diamond faces are warm, but they have a strong **will**.

     People with rectangular faces control their feelings, but they are intelligent and **creative**. These people work hard and are very reliable. Their work is

20 very important to them and comes before everything else, even family. They are not easy to be around when they do not feel free or when they feel bored. Many people with rectangular faces are at their best when they are older.

     Square faces usually belong to men, but women can also have them. Men with this kind of face are good at making decisions and keeping to them.

25 They are **generous** and honest. They put their friends first in everything. Both men and women with square faces are lucky and live a long life.

     A wide forehead, high cheekbones, and a pointed chin make a triangular face. People with triangular faces are lively and intelligent and often stand out from others; however, they worry too much and their emotions are

30 **fragile**, so they can get depressed easily. Because of this, they do better in jobs where they work with people.

The Chinese believe that a person with a wide jaw and narrow forehead is like the Earth and changes little. People with this kind of face love success and will almost always get what they want, especially money and all that
35 it brings. A man with this kind of face will not be close to his children, but his children will respect his strength. A woman with this kind of face was Jacqueline Kennedy, who had a strong character even in difficult times.

People with wide foreheads and square chins are intelligent and work hard to get what they want. They can be calm and quiet, or they can be the
40 opposite, too, because they like to get attention. Famous movie people like Paul Newman and Jane Fonda have this kind of face; so did Picasso, the painter. They usually have a long life and save their energy for important times in life.

People with wide foreheads and high cheekbones show strong character
45 and a lot of energy. This helps them to be normal again if something bad happens. They know what they like and don't like to change their habits. Nevertheless, they like to live a full life.

Vocabulary

A. Vocabulary in Context

Complete the sentences with the following words.

cheekbones	fragile	jaw
confident	generous	will
creative		

1. Some people have a wide ___jaw___, which makes their face look wide.
2. Women with high _cheekbones_ look attractive.
3. People with a strong ___will___ are able to do what they have to do.
4. Artists are ___creative___ people.
5. People with ___fragile___ emotions can get hurt very easily.
6. People with square faces are ___generous___ with their time and money.
7. People with round faces are ___confident___ and walk with their heads held up high.

B. Vocabulary in New Context

Answer these questions with complete sentences.

1. Who in the class has a big jaw?

Maria has a big jaw

2. Who in the class has high cheekbones?

Arel has hight cheekbones

3. Who is a creative person you know?

My best friend is a creature person.

4. When are you generous with money?
hào phóng

I am generous with money when people are in need

5. What are some objects in a house that are fragile?

glasses,

C. Vocabulary Building

Complete the sentences with the words from the box.

to characterize (verb)	character (noun)	characteristic (adj.)

1. His face has a _characteristic_ wide jaw, which tells us he gets what he wants.

2. You can tell her _character_ from her face.

to create (*verb*)	creativity (*noun*)	creative (*adj.*)

3. I don't want _____ a problem by asking for this.

4. You can tell her _____ by just looking around her room.

to prefer (*verb*)	preference (*noun*)	preferable (*adj.*)

5. I live so far away that it is _____ for me to work from home a few days a week.

6. If you are going to offer her a beverage, I know she has a _____ for tea.

Reading Comprehension

A. Looking for the Main Ideas

Circle the letter of the best answer.

1. The Chinese believe that the shape of the face _____b_____.
   a. is not important
   b. can show the character of a person
   c. is important when you want to be a movie star
   d. can show that a person has medical problems

2. The Chinese believe that there are _____a_____.
   a. eight basic shapes of faces
   b. square faces and round faces only
   c. some good shapes and some bad shapes
   d. four basic shapes of faces

3. The Chinese believe that the shape of your face can show _____b_____.
   a. when accidents will happen to you
   b. if you are intelligent
   c. if you are Chinese
   d. if you will have children

B. Looking for Details

Circle **T** if the sentence is true. Circle **F** if the sentence is false.

1. The Chinese believe that it is lucky to meet a person with a diamond face. **(T)** **F**

2. Jacqueline Kennedy had a square face.   T   (F)

3. The Chinese believe that round faces are intelligent.   (T)   F

4. Jane Fonda has a rectangular face.   T   (F)

5. The Chinese believe that people with triangular faces can get depressed easily.   (T)   F

6. The Chinese believe that people with diamond faces are not lucky in love.   T   (F)

Discussion Questions

Discuss the answers to these questions with your classmates.

1. Do you think there is any truth in reading people's faces (physiognomy)? How reliable is it?

2. Ask the students in your class which part of the face helps them understand a person's character. Fill out the questionnaire below.

Name	Country	Shape of Face	Shape of Eyes	Shape of Mouth	Shape of Ears	Other

3. Discuss what shapes of face, eyes, mouth, ears, etc., show good character.

Critical Thinking Questions

Discuss the answers to these questions with your classmates.

1. According to the reading, people with round faces and square faces live long lives. Do you think this is true? Why or why not? What things do you think help people live long lives?

2. Do you believe in luck? Do you believe that some people are naturally luckier than others? Why or why not? Do you know some people who seem to be lucky? Who are they?

Writing

Writing Skills

A. Organizing: Joining Compound Sentences with *and*, *but*, or *or*

A *compound sentence* is made by joining two simple sentences. These two simple sentences are joined by a *coordinating conjunction*. In this chapter, we will look at the coordinating conjunctions **and**, **but**, and **or**.

Using *and* to Join Two Sentences

We can use **and** to join two sentences that are alike or to join to a sentence another sentence that gives extra information.

Examples:

The Chinese believe that there are eight basic shapes of faces. Each shape shows a special character.

The Chinese believe that there are eight basic shapes of faces, **and** each shape shows a special character.

Note: Use a comma before **and**.

Using *but* to Join Two Sentences

We can use **but** to join two sentences that give opposite information or to join a positive sentence and a negative sentence that talk about the same subject:

+, but –
–, but +

Examples:

People with diamond faces may not be happy when they are young. They get what they want later in their lives.

People with diamond faces may not be happy when they are young, **but** they get what they want later in their lives.

Note: Use a comma before **but**.

Using *or* to Join Two Sentences

We can use **or** to join two sentences that give a choice or alternative.

Examples:

People with wide foreheads and square chins can be calm and quiet. They can be just the opposite, too.

People with wide foreheads and square chins can be calm and quiet, **or** they can be just the opposite, too.

Note: Use a comma before **or**.

We use a comma with **and**, **but**, or **or** only in compound sentences. When we use **and**, **but**, or **or** in a simple sentence, we do not use a comma. In a sentence, **and**, **but**, or **or** can join two nouns, two adjectives, two adverbs, or two verbs.

Examples:

1. Two nouns joined by **and**:
Both <u>men</u> and <u>women</u> with square faces are lucky.
     (noun)   (noun)

2. Two adjectives joined by **and**:
They are <u>intelligent</u> and <u>creative</u>.
   (adjective)   (adjective)

3. Two nouns joined by **or**:
A face may look round because of a small <u>forehead</u> or <u>chin</u>.
    (noun)   (noun)

4. Two adjectives joined by **or**:
They are not easy to be around when they feel <u>bored</u> or <u>not free</u>.
    (adjective)   (adjective)

Compare the sentences you just read with the compound sentences you have studied. Now underline all the coordinating conjunctions (**and**, **but**, and **or**) in the reading passage. Notice the punctuation with simple and compound sentences.

B. Exercises

1. Use the conjunction in parentheses to join the two sentences into a compound sentence. Use the correct punctuation.

1. Almost all the Chinese emperors had round faces. Many famous explorers had them, too. (and)

Example: <u>Almost all the Chinese emperors had round faces, and many famous explorers had them, too.</u>

2. People with triangular faces may not be tall. They look tall because of the shape of their face. (but)

_____

_____

3. These people are confident. They will usually live a long life. (and)

_____

_____

4. Some may be movie stars. They may work as flight attendants. (or)

_____

_____

5. People with high cheekbones know what they want. It is hard to make them change their minds. (and)

_____

_____

6. People with this shape of face may often be leaders. They may also be criminals. (but)

_____

_____

7. They can control their feelings. They are intelligent and creative. (but)

_____

_____

8. Square faces usually belong to men. Women can have them, too. (but)

_____

_____

2. Write compound sentences with **and**, **but**, or **or**. First think of two complete sentences. Then join them with **and**, **but**, or **or**. Do not forget to punctuate.

1. Write a compound sentence about a characteristic of a person's face. Use the word **and** to join the parts of your compound sentence.

Example: _My grandfather has big ears with big ear lobes, and everybody says he will live for a long time._

_____

_____

2. Write a compound sentence about a person's face. Use the word **but**.

Example: _Uncle Joe has a red face, but he does not have a bad temper._

_____

_____

3. Write a compound sentence about a person's face. Use the word **or**.

Example: _Tony looks pale, or he may just be tired._

_____

_____

3. Find the mistakes. There are 10 mistakes in grammar, punctuation, and capitalization. Find and correct them.

People with a wide forehead, and high cheekbones have a face that looks solid, and bony. Famous example of people with this *These* face are christopher columbus, greta garbo and ludwig beethoven.

Writing Practice

A. Rewrite a Paragraph

Here, you will rewrite a paragraph following the rules you have learned in this unit. In Unit 2, you will be writing your own paragraphs.

Work alone or with a friend. The paragraph below has some mistakes. Rewrite the paragraph. Make sure you do these things:

1. Write a title.
2. Indent the first line.
3. Join the sentences with the correct word from the parentheses.
4. Check for capital letters, periods, and commas.

eyes are a very important part of the Face. Your eyes will tell people your real feelings. When a person smiles, check his or her eyes for smile lines (and/but) a warm expression. The lips can lie in a smile (but/and/or) the eyes cannot lie. Your pupils* get bigger or smaller. when you look at the light, they get bigger (but/and) when you look at the dark they get smaller. your pupils also get bigger when you look at something you like (and) they get smaller when you look at something you do not like. So light-colored eyes are easier to read (and/or) dark eyes are a mystery.

> Note: The pupil is the small, black, round part in the center of the colored part of your eye.

B. Write Your Final Copy

After you check your work, you can handwrite your final copy on paper or use a computer.

Weaving It Together

⏱ Timed Writing

Choose a person you know. Write the person's name or relationship to you (for example, "My Brother") as your title. Write 5 sentences about what this person looks like and his or her character. Write your sentences to form a paragraph. Don't forget to indent the first line. You have 50 minutes.

Connecting to the Internet

A. Use the Internet to look up these famous left-handed people: Queen Victoria, Barack Obama, David Rockefeller, H. G. Wells, Buzz Aldrin, Nicole Kidman, Bill Gates, David Bowie, and Pablo Picasso.
- What is each person famous for?
- Other than being left-handed, which of these people have something in common?
- Which ones have traits that are common to left-brained people? Which ones don't?

B. Physiognomy is deciding a person's character based on their face. Phrenology uses something else to understand a person's character. Use the Internet to look up *phrenology*. Which Website gave you the most information to answer the following questions?
- What is phrenology?
- Who started this study and when?
- At what time in history was it most popular?
- What did a phrenologist do to find out about a person's character?

What Do You Think Now?

Refer to page 1 at the beginning of this unit. Do you know the answers now? Complete the sentence, or circle the best answer.

1. _____ percent of the population is left-handed.
2. Intelligent people (have/don't have) heavier brains.
3. (Right/Left)-handed people are generally good at math, and they are practical and safe.
4. The Chinese believe there are _____ basic shapes of the face.
5. The Chinese (believe/don't believe) the diamond shape is one of the shapes of the face.

Food

What Do You Think?

Answer the questions with your best guess. Circle **Yes** or **No**.

Do you think . . .

1. potatoes originally came from Europe?	**Yes**	**No**
2. potatoes were the main food in Ireland at one time?	**Yes**	**No**
3. the Germans loved potatoes from the first time they saw them?	**Yes**	**No**
4. in parts of Asia, people think fish heads are the tastiest part of fish?	**Yes**	**No**
5. there are special restaurants that serve only snakes?	**Yes**	**No**

Chapter 3

Live a Little: Eat Potatoes!

Pre-Reading

Discuss the answers to these questions with your classmates.

1. How do you like to eat potatoes?
2. How often do you eat potatoes?
3. What do you eat french fries with?
4. What do you see on the baked potato?
5. Which type of potato do you prefer to eat? Why?

Key Vocabulary

Do you know these words? Match the words with the meanings.

1. imagine __b__
2. instead __d__
3. poison __h__
4. disease __a__
5. advantage __g__
6. baked __f__
7. invented __c__
8. dish __e__

a. a sickness
b. have a picture in your mind about something
c. thought of or made for the first time
d. in place of
e. special cooked food of some kind
f. cooked in the oven
g. something that is helpful or useful
h. something that can kill you if you eat or drink it

Live a Little: Eat Potatoes!

1   Can you **imagine** life without french fries? Potatoes are very popular today. They are the fourth most important crop in the world, after wheat, rice, and corn. But in the past, potatoes were not always popular. People in Europe started to eat them only 200 years ago!

5   In the 1500s, the Spanish went to South America to look for gold. There, they found people eating potatoes. The people of Peru in South America had been eating potatoes for 7,000 years! The Spanish brought the potato back to Europe with them. But people in Europe did not like this strange vegetable. Some people thought that if you ate potatoes, your skin would look like the

10   skin of a potato. Other people could not believe that you ate the underground part of the plant, so they ate the leaves **instead**. This made them sick because there is **poison** in the leaves. Others grew potatoes for their flowers. At one time in France, potato flowers were one of the most expensive flowers. Marie Antoinette, the wife of King Louis XVI, wore potato flowers in her hair.

15   Around 1780, the people of Ireland started to eat potatoes. They found that potatoes had many **advantages**. The potato grew on poor land, and it grew well in their cold and rainy climate. It gave more food than any other plant, and it needed little work. All they had to do was to plant the potatoes, and then they could do other work on the farm. On a small piece of land,

20   a farmer could grow enough potatoes to feed his family. A person could eat 8 to 10 pounds of potatoes a day, with some milk or cheese, and be very healthy. Soon, potatoes became the main food in Ireland. Then, in 1845, a **disease** killed all the potatoes in Ireland. Two million people died of hunger. Many Irish who did not die came to the United States at this time. Over a

25   million Irish came to America; one of them was the great-grandfather of John F. Kennedy.

In other parts of Europe, people did not want to change their old food habits. Some preferred to die of hunger rather than eat potatoes. In 1774, King Frederick of Germany wanted to stop his people from dying of hunger.

30   He understood that potatoes were a good food, so he told the people to plant
      and eat potatoes or else his men would cut off their noses. The people were
      not happy, but they had no choice and so started to eat potatoes. Today,
      people in this part of Germany eat more potatoes than any other nationality.
      Each person eats about 370 pounds of potatoes every year!

35   Today, many countries have their own potato **dishes**. Germans eat potato
      salad, and the United States has the **baked** potato. And, of course, the French
      invented french fries. Now french fries are popular all over the world. The
      English eat them with salt and vinegar, the French eat them with salt and
      pepper, the Belgians eat them with mayonnaise, and the Americans eat them
40   with ketchup.

Vocabulary

A. Vocabulary in Context

Complete the sentences with the following words.

advantage	dishes	invented
baked	imagine	poison
disease	instead	

1. We cannot ___imagine___ eating a hamburger without french fries.
2. Some plants have ___poison___ in them and can kill you if you eat them.
3. People didn't grow potatoes for food; they grew them for their flowers
   ___instead___.
4. The potato got a ___disease___, which killed the plants.
5. Americans cook the potato with its skin in the oven. They call it a
   ___baked___ potato.
6. From the name, we know that the French ___invented___ french fries.
7. There are many ___dishes___ you can make with potatoes.
8. The potato has one big _____ over other crops—it is easy to
   grow.

Word Partnership	Use **imagine** with:
v.	can/can't/could/couldn't imagine *something*, **try to** imagine
adj.	**difficult/easy/hard/impossible to** imagine

B. Vocabulary in New Context

Answer the questions with complete sentences.

1. What is your favorite baked food?

My favorite baked food is chicken.

2. What would you eat instead of potatoes?

I would eat rice and vegetables instead of potato

3. What is your favorite dish when you eat at home?

My favorite dish is steak when I eat at home.

4. What is one advantage of learning English?

5. What is a disease that is a problem today?

HIV is a disease that is a problem today

6. What animal or plant has poison?

Snake has poison.

C. Vocabulary Building

Complete the sentences with the words from the box.

| to imagine (*verb*) | imagination (*noun*) | imaginative (*adj.*) |

1. He wrote a very _____ story.
2. It's difficult _____ a world without computers.

| to invent (*verb*) | invention (*noun*) | inventive (*adj.*) |

3. John is very _____ in the kitchen, and the food doesn't always taste bad.
4. Ketchup is a great _____.

| to choose (*verb*) | choice (*noun*) | choosy (*adj.*) |

5. Amy is very _____ about her food. *wishy*
6. There were so many dishes, it was difficult for me _____.

Reading Comprehension

A. Looking for the Main Ideas

Circle the letter of the best answer.

1. Potatoes are _____.
   a. popular today
   b. not popular today
   c. popular only in America
   d. popular only in Europe

2. In the 1500s, people in Europe _____.
   a. liked the potato
   b. had bad skin
   c. did not like the potato as food
   d. invented french fries

3. In about 1780, people started to _____.
   a. eat potatoes in Ireland
   b. grow potatoes for their flowers
   c. go to Peru
   d. die of hunger in America

4. French fries are _____.
   a. a special dish in Belgium
   b. popular all over the world
   c. from Germany
   d. most popular in America

B. Looking for Details

One word in each sentence is not correct. Rewrite the sentence with the correct word.

1. Potatoes grew in Europe 7,000 years ago.

   Peru

   _____

   _____

2. In the 1700s, the Spanish brought the potato back to Europe.

   _1500s_

   _____

   _____

3. There is poison in the skin of the potato.

   _____

   _____

4. A disease killed the people in Ireland in 1845.

   _____

   _____

5. Five million people died of hunger in Ireland.

   _____

   _____

6. The potato dish of Germany is the baked potato.

   _____

   _____

7. The Americans invented french fries.

   _____

   _____

Discussion Questions

Discuss the answers to these questions with your classmates.

1. Find out from the students in your class about the main food and drink in their country. Fill out the chart below.

Name	Country	Main Food	Main Drink
Ana	Mexico	tortillas	coffee

2. Is the main drink in your country good for you? Why or why not?

3. In your country, are there any customs related to the main food?

Critical Thinking Questions

Discuss the answers to these questions with your classmates.

1. In what places in the world today do people suffer because they don't have enough food? What are some causes? What can be done to avoid this problem?

2. What plants, besides the potato, are easy to grow and healthy for people to eat? What kinds of foods are made from these crops? What foods are best for good health? What foods are not as healthy?

Writing

Writing Model

topic sentence: topic + controlling idea
→*supporting details*
conclusion

Now read the following paragraph written by a student. Can you guess where the student is from?

Bread

1   In my country, bread is an important part of our everyday food. When we sit down for a meal, there is always bread on the table. For breakfast, we have bread with butter or cheese. Some people have jam or olives. For lunch, we have bread with a meat or vegetable dish. Poor people eat more bread

5   with a small piece of meat or vegetable or cheese. For example, the lunch of a worker may be a loaf of bread with some yogurt. Again at dinner, we eat bread with whatever food there is on the table. When there is rice, we have bread, too. We think that if there is no bread, there is no food.

Writing Skills

Organizing: The Topic Sentence

Underline the first sentence in the model paragraph above. It is the topic sentence.

The *topic sentence* is the most important sentence in a paragraph. It tells the reader what the paragraph is about, or its main idea. The topic sentence is usually the first sentence in a paragraph. The topic sentence has two parts: the topic and the controlling idea. The *topic* is the subject of your paragraph. It is what you are writing about.

Example:

Bread is an important part of our everyday food.

Topic: Bread

Exercise

1. Circle the topic in these sentences.

    1. Potatoes are good for you.
    2. There are many kinds of rice.
    3. The hamburger is a popular food in America.
    4. People all around the world drink tea.
    5. Bread is the poor man's food.

The *controlling idea* limits or controls your topic to the one aspect that you want to write about.

Example:

    Rice   plays an important part in some ceremonies.
    (topic)   (controlling idea)

or

    Rice   is a nutritious part of our diet.
    (topic)   (controlling idea)

  A topic can have more than one controlling idea. You could write one paragraph about how rice plays an important part in some ceremonies, a second paragraph about how rice is a nutritious part of our diet, and a third paragraph about another aspect of rice. There are many possibilities.

Exercise

2. Underline the controlling idea in these topic sentences.

    1. Bread is an important part of our diet.
    2. Bread plays an important part in our religion.
    3. Potatoes are easy to grow.
    4. Potatoes are the basic food of the Irish.
    5. French fries are popular all over the world.

Topic sentences are often opinions. A simple fact is not a good topic sentence, because there is nothing more you can say about it. If a topic sentence is an opinion, then you can write a paragraph about it.

Exercise

3. Work with a partner. Decide which sentence, *a* or *b*, is a fact.

1. a. Rice is a cereal.
b. In some countries, people eat too much rice.

2. a. The potato is a vegetable.
b. Potatoes are good for you.

3. a. Rice contains starch.
b. Rice should be cooked in a special pot.

4. a. Drinking coffee helps you concentrate.
b. Coffee is made from coffee beans.

5. a. Chewing gum is good for you.
b. Chewing gum is made from plastic and rubber.

6. a. Coffee contains caffeine.
b. The best coffee comes from Colombia.

Another kind of topic sentence divides the topic into different parts.

Examples:

1. Potatoes are good for you in <u>three ways</u>.
2. There are <u>four basic methods</u> of eating french fries.
3. Potato eaters fall into <u>different groups</u>.

When you use this kind of topic sentence, you need to support it by talking about the different parts. For example, to support sentence 1, you would write about the three ways potatoes are good for you.

Exercises

4. Put a checkmark (✓) in the box if the sentence is a good topic sentence.

☐ **1.** Bread is made from flour.
☒ **2.** Drinking too much coffee may be dangerous for you in several ways.
☒ **3.** In some countries, people have very different ideas about drinking tea.
☐ **4.** Potatoes are a root vegetable.

☒ **5.** Rice is the basic food for half of the world's population.

☐ **6.** Potatoes contain many nutrients.

☒**7.** Rice may be cooked in four ways.

5. Find the mistakes. There are 10 mistakes in grammar, capitalization, and spelling. Find and correct them.

The incas at south america grow potatoes for thousands of years before the spanish arrived. The potatoe was the main part of their diet and culture. The incas measured time by how long it took to cook potatoes. They also used potatoes to tell their Fortune. If they found an odd number of potatoes, it was bad luck. If they found a even number, it was good luck.

Writing Practice

A. Write a Paragraph

Choose one of the topics below:

1. The main food in my country
2. The main drink in my country

B. Pre-Write

Work with a group, a partner, or alone.

1. Write your topic at the top of your paper. (Say what your main food or drink is.)
2. Then ask a question about your topic. This will help you to get ideas. Choose one of these question words:
   - Who?
   - What? / In what way?
   - Where?
   - When?
   - Why?

Example:

Rice is an important food in my country.

Question: Why?

3. Write down as many answers as you can. If you find that the question word does not work, try another question word.

C. Outline

1. Organize your ideas.

Step 1: Write a topic sentence.

Step 2: Choose some of the answers to your question to use as supporting sentences.

2. Make a more detailed outline. The paragraph outline below will help you.

Paragraph Outline

(Topic sentence) _____.
(Supporting fact) _____.
(Supporting fact) _____.
(Supporting fact) _____.
(Concluding sentence) _____.

D. Write a Rough Draft

Using the outline you made, write a rough draft of your paragraph.

E. Revise Your Rough Draft

Using the checklist below, check your rough draft or let your partner check it.

Paragraph Checklist

- ☐ Did you give your paragraph a title?
- ☐ Did you indent the first line?
- ☐ Did you write on every other line? (Look at pages 8 and 9 for instructions on paragraph form.)
- ☐ Does your paragraph have a topic sentence?
- ☐ Does your topic sentence have a controlling idea?
- ☐ Do your other sentences support your topic sentence?
- ☐ Are your ideas in the correct order?
- ☐ Does your paragraph have a concluding sentence?

F. Edit Your Paragraph

Work with a partner or your teacher to edit your paragraph. Check spelling, punctuation, vocabulary, and grammar. Use the editing checklist below.

Editing Checklist

- ☐ Subject in every sentence?
- ☐ Verb in every sentence?
- ☐ Words in correct order?
- ☐ Sentences begin with a capital letter?
- ☐ Sentences end with a period directly at the end of a sentence?
- ☐ Sentences have a space between them?
- ☐ Commas in the correct place?
- ☐ Wrong words?
- ☐ Spelling?
- ☐ Missing words (use insertion mark: ^)?

G. Write Your Final Copy

When your rough draft has been edited, you can write the final copy of your paragraph.

Chapter

Bugs, Rats, and Other Tasty Dishes

Pre-Reading

Discuss the answers to these questions with your classmates.

1. What kinds of food do you see in the picture?
2. Which of these foods would you like to eat?
3. What other foods of this kind do people eat?

Key Vocabulary

Do you know these words? Match the words with the meanings.

1. delicacy ___c___
2. alive ___d___
3. pork ___g___
4. grilled ___h___
5. appetizer ___f___
6. native ___b___
7. dessert ___a___
8. paste ___e___

a. the last part of a meal, usually a sweet dish
b. original to a land
c. a special food that is expensive or hard to find
d. not dead
e. a soft, smooth cream
f. a small amount of food served before the main meal
g. cooked on metal bars over a fire
h. meat from a pig

Reading

Sâu to, côn trùng   con chuột cống

Bugs, Rats, and Other Tasty Dishes

con rệp

1 **W**ould you like some chicken feet? How about frogs' legs? Well, you can't say no to a 50-year-old egg! It's a **delicacy** that people pay a lot of money for, believe it or not. People in different parts of the world eat just about everything, from elephants' trunks to monkeys' brains.

5 Chicken feet are a favorite **appetizer** in China, while in Taiwan turkey feet are a favorite. In Taiwan, people have both chicken feet and turkey feet in their salads. Whereas Americans like the white meat of a chicken, people in Taiwan prefer other parts of the chicken, like the dark meat and the inside parts. They often deep-fry the skin and serve it separately, along with the
10 main meal.

Snakes and eels are delicacies in most parts of the world. In France and England, fish shops sell eels that are **alive**. In Asia, there are special restaurants for eating snakes. Everything on the menu is snake: snake soup, snake appetizers, snake main course, and snake **desserts**! When you go to
15 the restaurant, the snakes are alive. You choose the snake you want to eat. Then the waiter kills the snake before your very eyes!

People line up in front of restaurants in Malaysia, Singapore, Thailand, and Indonesia to get fish heads. The restaurants prepare the whole fish, but people start by eating the head, which they believe is the tastiest part of the
20 fish. So many people ask for fish heads that the price of fish heads is higher than the price of the best steak.

What about eating a fish that can kill you? The Japanese put their lives in danger every time they eat this delicacy. The fish is called the blowfish, and it is very poisonous. Although they know that they could die, they continue
25 to eat it. Every year, the Japanese eat 20,000 tons of blowfish, and 70 to 100 people die from it every year.

Rats and mice are also a special food in some parts of the world. In China, people like rice rats especially. They clean and salt them and leave

them in oil. Then they hang them to dry. These rats sell in the market for
30   twice the price of the best **pork**. Farmers in Thailand and the Philippines
also love rice rats. In Vietnam, mice from the rice fields are fried or **grilled**.
In Spain, there is a traditional dish called paella, which is made with rice
and pieces of fish. In the town of Valencia, this dish also has rat meat to give
it a special flavor.

35   Insects like termites, ants, and bees are delicacies to many people. In
Africa, people fight over termite nests. They eat the termites alive and say
that they taste like pineapple. In India, people make the ants into a **paste**
and eat them with curry. In Borneo, people mix ants with rice. They say
that the ants give the rice a special flavor. In Australia, the **native** people
40   drink ants. They mash them in water and say that the drink tastes like
lemonade! And bees are delicious when you fry them. You just can't stop
eating them!

Vocabulary

A. Vocabulary in Context

Complete the sentences with the words below.

alive	dessert	paste
appetizer	grilled	pork
delicacy	native	

1. People pay lot of money for a ___delicacy___ like a 50-year-old egg.
2. In some fish shops, they sell fish that are not dead but ___alive___.
3. Meat can be ___grilled___ over a fire.
4. In Asia, people have pigs for ___pork___.
5. In Asia, snake can be an ___appetizer___ before the main meal.
6. The ___native___ people of Australia are the Aborigines.
7. It's nice to have a sweet ___dessert___ after the main meal.
8. Sometimes, people make ants into a ___paste___ like a cream.

B. Vocabulary in New Context

Answer these questions with complete sentences.

1. What is a favorite appetizer in your country?

Vegetables are   favorite appetizer in my country

2. What is your favorite dessert?

Ice-cream is my favorite dessert

3. What food do you like grilled?

I like grilled chicken

4. What plant or animal is native to your country?

5. What kinds of food do people make with pork?

6. What food comes in a paste?

7. What is a delicacy you like or don't like?

I like lobster

C. Vocabulary Building

Complete the sentences with the words from the box.

to endanger (*verb*)	danger (*noun*)	dangerous (*adj.*)

1. It is _____ to walk in that part of town at night.
2. There is a _____ when you eat blowfish. You can die!

to specialize (*verb*)	specialty (*noun*)	special (*adj.*)

3. Paella is the _____ of that restaurant.
4. The restaurant makes a _____ sauce for the steak.

to live (*verb*)	life (*noun*)	alive (*adj.*)

5. We eat _____, but some people live to eat.
6. I cannot eat food that is _____.

Reading Comprehension

A. Looking for the Main Ideas

Circle the letter of the best answer.

1. People in different parts of the world eat _____.
   a. only frogs' legs
   b. just about everything
   c. only legs, brains, and eggs
   d. mostly insects and snakes

2. In most parts of the world, snakes and eels are _____.
   a. delicacies
   b. only appetizers
   c. not found in shops or restaurants
   d. desserts

3. Insects are _____.
   a. good only with lemonade
   b. special in pineapple
   c. delicious to many people
   d. popular in Africa only

B. Looking for Details

Circle **T** if the sentence is true. Circle **F** if the sentence is false.

hw

1. In Asia, there are special restaurants for eating snakes.   **T**   F
2. In Australia, they mash ants in rice.   T   **F**
3. In India, people make ants into a soup.   T   **F**
4. Some people say that bees are delicious when you fry them.   **T**   F
5. In Africa, people say that ants taste like eels.   T   **F**
6. Some people pay a lot of money for old eggs.   **T**   F

Discussion Questions

Discuss the answers to these questions with your classmates.

1. Do you know about any other strange foods that people eat?
2. Did you ever eat a kind of food that was strange for you? What was it like?
3. Describe a delicacy that people eat in your country.

Critical Thinking Questions

Discuss the answers to these questions with your classmates.

1. Just thinking about a certain food sometimes makes one feel sick. But another person will say that food is delicious! Why is this? Why do we eat the things we do? Where do we get our ideas about what tastes good or bad?
2. Some people believe that by eating an animal's brains, they will become smarter. Others believe that eating a heart gives them more courage. Do you believe this is true? Why or why not? How do these beliefs cause problems for some of the world's endangered animals? Should there be laws against eating some animal parts? Why or why not?

Writing

Writing Model

Now read the following paragraph written by a student. Can you guess where the student is from?

A Specialty in My Country

1   The people in my country make a special dish from the izote flower, which is delicious to eat. The flower grows on top of a beautiful tree. You can see these trees in the gardens of houses. You can also buy izote flowers in the market. The best time for the flower is in the summer, from November to
5   March. From the flowers we make a special dish that we eat almost every week in the summer. To prepare this dish, we boil the petals of the flower in water with salt and garlic. Then we take out the petals and add them to beaten eggs. We fry this mixture like an omelet. When it is ready, we eat it with tomato sauce. The izote flower is a special flower in my country.

Writing Skills

A. Organizing: *The Supporting Sentences and Concluding Sentence*

The first sentence in the model paragraph is the topic sentence. The next sentences are supporting sentences. The last sentence is the concluding sentence.

Supporting Sentences

Supporting sentences tell more about the topic introduced in the topic sentence. Supporting sentences give the reader more facts about or examples of the topic.

Example:

Topic sentence: The people in my country make a special dish from the izote flower.

Supporting sentences:
Where the flower grows

Where you can buy the flower

When you can buy the flower

When you eat the dish

How you make it

How you eat it

Exercise

1. Look at the following groups of sentences. The topic sentence is underlined. All except for one of the sentences in each group support the topic sentence. Find the sentence that does **not** support the topic sentence. Circle the letter of your answer.

   1. The carambola is a popular fruit in Taiwan.
      a. It is not expensive.
      b. You can buy it in any supermarket or fruit store in my country.
      c. It is good for you when you are sick.
      d. Most Americans do not like the carambola.

   2. The platano, which looks like a banana, has many uses in my country, Peru.
      a. It is an export for my country.
      b. It is used in many kinds of dishes.
      c. Bananas are also a favorite.
      d. It is a supplement for milk.

   3. Ginger is a traditional seasoning in China.
      a. It is used in many traditional dishes.
      b. The Chinese have used ginger for a long time.
      c. It is an old custom to use ginger when the dish has a strong smell.
      d. Ginger is expensive in the United States.

4. <u>Soya beans are becoming popular all over the world.</u>

      a. They have always been popular in Asia.

      b. They are easy to grow.

      (c.) They are not as good as meat.

      d. They have a high food value.

The Concluding Sentence

The last sentence in your paragraph is called the *concluding sentence*. This sentence tells the reader it is the end of the paragraph.

The concluding sentence and the topic sentence are similar. They are both general sentences. You can write the concluding sentence like the topic sentence, but use different words.

Two ways to write a concluding sentence are to

1. say the topic sentence in different words.

or

2. summarize the main points in the paragraph.

Many concluding sentences begin with one of these phrases:

      In conclusion, . . .
      In summary, . . .

Exercises

2. Write a concluding sentence for each of the topic sentences below.

Example:

Topic sentence: Kimchi is an indispensable side dish at meals in Korea.

Concluding sentence: In conclusion, there is no day without *kimchi* on the table in my country, Korea.

1. In Japan, we use seaweed [*song biến*] in many of our traditional meals.

    <u>In summary, seaweed is very popular in Japan</u>

2. Americans eat turkey on two of their traditional holidays.

_____

_____

3. In many countries, it is usual to eat food with hot peppers.

_____

_____

4. Beans play an important part in Brazilian food.

_____

_____

5. The French like to eat cheese and have over 300 different cheeses.

_____

_____

3. Find the mistakes. There are 10 mistakes in grammar, punctuation, capitalization, and spelling. Find and correct them.

We all know that muslims don't eat porks but many people don't know that in pakistan they never offer beef to a important guest. Beef is cheap and easily available, so a pakistani would never offer a guest something as common as steak. Instead, he or she would serve leg of lam as an appetize and chicken, or fish as main course or the other way around.

Writing Practice

A. **Write a Paragraph**

Choose a specialty or delicacy in your country.

B. Pre-Write

Work with a group, a partner, or alone.

1. Write the name of a specialty or delicacy in your country (the topic).
2. Now write a controlling idea about the topic. (Say why it is important/special/ traditional.)
3. Then ask questions about your controlling idea. Use some of the following question words: When? Where? Who? How? Why?

Example:

A traditional food in my country is bean sprout soup.

Questions: When do you eat it?

How do you make it?

Why do people eat it?

C. Outline

1. Organize your ideas.

   Step 1: Write a topic sentence.

   Step 2: Choose some of the answers to your question to use as supporting sentences.

2. Make a more detailed outline. The paragraph outline will help you.

Paragraph Outline

(Topic sentence)   _____.
(Supporting sentence 1)   _____.
(Supporting sentence 2)   _____.
(Supporting sentence 3)   _____.
(Supporting sentence 4)   _____.
(Concluding sentence)   _____.

D. Write a Rough Draft

Using the outline you made, write a rough draft of your paragraph.

E. Revise Your Rough Draft

Using the paragraph checklist below, check your rough draft or let your partner check it.

Paragraph Checklist

- ☐ Did you give your paragraph a title?
- ☐ Did you indent the first line?
- ☐ Did you write on every other line?
- ☐ Does your paragraph have a topic sentence?
- ☐ Does your topic sentence have a controlling idea?
- ☐ Do your other sentences support your topic sentence?
- ☐ Are your ideas in the correct order?
- ☐ Does your paragraph have a concluding sentence?

F. Edit Your Paragraph

Work with a partner or your teacher to edit your paragraph. Check spelling, punctuation, vocabulary, and grammar. Use the editing checklist below.

Editing Checklist

- ☐ Subject in every sentence?
- ☐ Verb in every sentence?
- ☐ Words in correct order?
- ☐ Sentences begin with a capital letter?
- ☐ Sentences end with a period directly at the end of a sentence?
- ☐ Sentences have a space between them?
- ☐ Commas in the correct place?
- ☐ Wrong words?
- ☐ Spelling?
- ☐ Missing words (use insertion mark: ^)?

G. Write Your Final Copy

When your rough draft has been edited, you can write the final copy of your paragraph.

Weaving It Together

⏱ Timed Writing

Choose a special food or delicacy you have not already written about in "Writing Practice." You have 50 minutes to write a paragraph.

Connecting to the Internet

A. Rice and corn feed people around the world. Choose either rice or corn and look up its history on the Internet. Which Website gave you the most information to answer the following questions?
- Who discovered this food?
- Where and when was it discovered?
- What kinds of food are made from it?
- What countries eat this food as part of their typical diet?

B. Use the Internet to find out where people eat these delicacies: bats, goat's head, jellied blood, jellied cow's foot, monkey toes, pig blood, sheep's head, and squirrel brain.

What Do You Think Now?

Refer to page 27 at the beginning of this unit. Do you know the answers now? Complete the sentence, or circle the best answer.

1. Potatoes originally came from _____.

2. Potatoes were/were not the main food in Ireland at one time.

3. The Germans loved/did not love potatoes from the first time they saw them.

4. In parts of Asia, people think _____ are the tastiest part of fish.

5. There are special restaurants that serve only _____.

Celebrations and Special Days

What Do You Think?

Answer the questions with your best guess. Circle **Yes** or **No**.

Do you think . . .

1. Nepal is an island?	**Yes**	**No**
2. the cow is important to Hindus?	**Yes**	**No**
3. people celebrate their brothers and sisters with a holiday?	**Yes**	**No**
4. Spanish-speaking countries have a special birthday for a girl, called a *quinceañera*, when she is 16?	**Yes**	**No**
5. The *quinceañera*, or special birthday, is only for the girl's family?	**Yes**	**No**

Chapter

5 Tihar: Festival of Lights

Pre-Reading

Discuss the answers to these questions with your classmates.

1. Why do you think the animal in the picture has garlands around its neck and horns?
2. For what celebrations or holidays do we use lights and decorations?
3. What kinds of things do we do when we have holidays and celebrations?

Key Vocabulary

Do you know these words? Match the words with the meanings.

1. holy ___b___
2. icon ___f___
3. mud ___e___
4. please ___g___
5. prosperity ___c___
6. stray ___h___
7. trail ___d___
8. worship ___a___

a. pray; show respect to God or gods
b. connected with religion
c. wealth; richness
d. leave signs behind as you move along
e. wet earth that is soft
f. a figure of a holy person
g. make happy
h. animal with no home

Reading

Track 5

Tihar: Festival of Lights

1   Tihar is one of the most important festivals for Hindus in Nepal. Nepal
is a small country between India and China. It has a population of about
23 million, most of whom are Hindu. The festival of Tihar takes place in late
autumn and lasts for five days. This festival is also called the festival of lights.

5   It is a time when all the houses light oil lamps, and the city is full of lights
and decorations. This festival is about worshipping different animals such as
the crow,[1] the dog, and the cow. During Tihar, the people also worship their
brothers and sisters and the goddess of wealth, Laxmi.

On the first day of the festival, people **worship** crows. Every family cooks

10   a delicious meal in the morning. Before they eat, each member of the family
puts some food on a plate of leaves and places it outside for the crows to eat.
People believe crows are the messenger of the Lord of Death. They worship
crows to keep sadness away.

The second day, people worship dogs. They decorate dogs with garlands of

15   flowers around their necks. They give dogs delicious food and put a red *tika*
(a special powder) on their foreheads. They even do this to **stray** dogs. It is
a day to respect all dogs. They pray for the dogs to guard their homes. Dogs
with garlands of flowers can be seen everywhere.

The third day is the most important day of the festival. Early in the

20   morning, people start to worship the cow. The cow is the symbol of wealth
and is the most **holy** animal for Hindus. They put *tika* on the cows' foreheads
and a garland of flowers around their necks. They give the cows nice things to
eat. People place the cows' manure in different parts of their houses. Later, in
the evening, they worship the goddess Laxmi. If people **please** the goddess,

25   she will give them wealth. People clean and decorate their houses. They put
oil lamps in every door and window. A female member of the family performs
a special ceremony or *puja*. She then puts a red **mud** footprint on the floor
entering the home and makes a **trail** to the room where the family worships

---

[1]**crow:** large, shiny black bird that makes a loud sound

the goddess. In this room, there are pictures and an **icon** of the goddess.
There is also a money box where each year the family puts money away for
the goddess. In the evening, girls go from door to door of their neighbors'
homes and sing songs of the goddess. They receive gifts in return.

The fourth day is a little different. The things people worship on this day
depend on their cultural background. Most people worship the ox. They
put *tika* on the oxen and a garland around their necks. They also give them
delicious food. Other people make a small hill out of cow manure, put some
grass on it, and perform a special ceremony, or *puja*, on it. Yet other people
worship themselves.

The fifth day is the day of brothers and sisters. Sisters wish their brothers
long life and **prosperity**. If you do not have a brother or sister, you can
make one of your relatives or friends a brother or a sister. On this day, sisters
will perform a *puja* and apply a special *tika* on their brothers. Then they put
garlands around their brothers and give them special gifts of food. Brothers in
return honor their sisters; they put garlands around their necks and give them
gifts of clothes and money.

This festival finally ends after five days of cooking, decorating, eating,
singing, dancing, shopping, relaxing, gift giving, and worshipping. There is
no doubt that Tihar is the most popular festival in Nepal.

Vocabulary

A. Vocabulary in Context

Complete these sentences with the following words.

5 an icon   3 please   7 trail
2 holy   8 prosperity   1 worship
6 mud   4 stray

1. During Tihar, people _____ animals, brothers and sisters, and the
   goddess Laxmi.
2. The cow is a _____ animal for Hindus.
3. People clean and decorate their homes to _____ the goddess.
4. On the second day, people worship dogs, even _____ dogs.
5. There is _____ of the goddess in a special room in people's
   homes.

6. A female member of the house puts a footprint made of red
_____ at the entrance of the house.

7. She makes a _____ from the entrance to the special room for
the goddess.

8. On the last day, sisters wish their brothers a long life and _____.

B. Vocabulary in New Context

Answer the questions with complete sentences.

1. In which season do you get mud?

we usually got mud when it is spring or fall

2. What places of worship do you most often see in your country?

I see churches and temples to worship in my country

3. What stray animals do you see sometimes?

Sometimes I see stray dogs and cats

4. What is one thing you do to please your mother or father?

In order to please my parents I would clean around my house

5. What item, do you think, is a sign of prosperity?

A luxury car

6. What is the name of a holy place or city?

Jerusalem is a holy place for many people

C. Vocabulary Building

Complete these sentences with the words from the box.

to please (verb)	pleasure (noun)	pleased (adj.)

1. It was a _____ to prepare the meal.

2. Are you _____ with the results of your test?

to prosper (verb)	prosperity (noun)	prosperous (adj.)

3. People follow many traditions for _____ in the new year.

4. The wide streets and large homes tell us this is a _____ area.

to decorate (verb)	decoration (noun)	decorative (adj.)

5. He wants _____ the bathroom this year.

6. Some people use _____ lights for the holidays.

Reading Comprehension

A. Looking for the Main Ideas

Circle the letter of the best answer.

1. The festival of Tihar is about _____.
   a. honoring the goddesses of light and wealth
   b. worshipping animals, people, and the goddess of wealth
   c. being kind to people and farm animals
   d. celebrating the flowers and foods of autumn

2. On the third day of the festival, people _____.
   a. perform ceremonies to please Laxmi
   b. clean their houses to prepare for guests
   c. worship cows by cleaning and washing them
   d. put lamps in windows to show they are wealthy

3. The fourth day is _____.

a. the only day set aside to honor relatives

b. only about the worship of the ox

c. different among various cultures

d. a day for cooking food and dancing

B. Looking for Details

Use complete sentences to answer the questions.

1. Who celebrates the festival of Tihar in Nepal?

2. Why do the people worship crows?

3. What do people pray for the dogs to do?

4. What is the cow the symbol of?

5. What does a female family member do on the third day of the festival?

6. What do brothers do to honor their sisters?

Discussion Questions

Discuss the answers to these questions with your classmates.

1. What are some important festivals or holidays in your country? What do people celebrate? How do they celebrate?

2. What is your favorite holiday? Why?

3. What holiday in another culture or country do you wish you celebrated in your country? Why?

Critical Thinking Questions

Discuss the answers to these questions with your classmates.

1. Why is it important for people to have festivals and holidays? What is their purpose? What do festivals and holidays do for a culture or country?

2. Why do you think that lights and candles are important to many festivals and holidays? What are lights a symbol of?

Writing

Writing Model

Now read the following paragraph written by a student. Can you guess where the student is from?

New Year in My Country

1   In my country, we call the New Year *Tet*. First, on the night the New Year begins, we go to the temple. We pray to Buddha, give thanks for the past year, and pray that the new year will be happy. Then we return home. Next, just before midnight, my father bows before an altar we have for our dead

5   relatives. He offers food to the relatives and invites them to join the family. At midnight, we have firecrackers, and children make a lot of noise. It is Tet. The New Year is here. Finally, we sit down and have a big and delicious dinner. We celebrate all night.

Writing Skills

A. Organizing: *Describing a Process*

When you want to tell about how you do something, like take a bath or wash your car, you must list the main steps. Make sure that the steps are in the correct order. Then to make the order clear to the reader, use the following words, which show time order:

> **First,** . . . (Second, . . . Third, . . .)
> **Next,** . . .
> **Then** . . .
> **Finally/Lastly,** . . .

These words come at the beginning of a sentence. Note that you use a comma (,) after each word except **then**. You do not need to use these words in each sentence of your paragraph.

Exercises

1. Underline the words that show time order in the model paragraph.
2. Put the following sentences in the correct order. Number them 1, 2, 3, 4, ...

1. To wash your hair, follow these steps.

_____ 2 _____ Put some shampoo on your hair.

_____ 1 _____ Wet your hair with water.

_____ 5 _____ Rinse off the shampoo.

_____ 3 _____ Lather your hair with shampoo.

_____ 6 _____ Dry your hair with a towel.

_____ 4 _____ Repeat the process.

2. Washing dishes is easy.

_____ 2 _____ Wash the plates in soapy water with a brush.

_____ 1 _____ Remove pieces of food from the plates.

_____ 4 _____ Dry the plates with a towel.

_____ 3 _____ Rinse off the soapy water.

3. Cleaning windows is not difficult.

_____ 2 _____ You need a bucket and a large sponge.

_____ 4 _____ Dry the windows with a paper towel.

_____ 3 _____ Wet the sponge, and wipe the windows with it.

_____ 1 _____ Fill the bucket with water and a little ammonia.

_____ 5 _____ Your windows will shine.

B. Punctuation: *Comma (,) with Items in a Series*

You use a comma to separate three or more items in a series. Do not use a comma if there are only two items.

Examples:

This festival finally ends after five days of cooking, decorating, eating, singing, dancing, shopping, relaxing, gift giving, and worshipping.

They have fun by playing games, singing, and dancing.

People clean and decorate their houses. (No comma needed.)

Nepal is between India and China. (No comma needed.)

You can make one of your friends a brother or a sister. (No comma needed.)

Exercises

3. Put commas in these sentences where necessary. Note that some sentences do not need a comma.

   1. People worship different animals such as the crow, the dog and the cow.
   2. Tihar takes place in late autumn and lasts for five days.
   3. It's a time to worship animals, brothers, and sisters and the goddess Laxmi.
   4. The city is full of lights and decorations.
   5. They put garlands around their neck give them special food and make them gifts.
   6. Sisters wish their brothers long life and prosperity.

4. Find the mistakes. There are 10 mistakes in punctuation, capitalization, and spelling. Find and correct them.

The Chinese New Year Celebration is 15 days long. The Chinese clean their homes and decorate two. They also buy new clothes and prepare plenty of food. The big celebration start on new year's eve. First, they have a big dinner with plenty of food. There are always special foods like a whole fish chicken and long noodles for long life. After dinner, the whole family sits up for the night. They play games, or watch television. Finally there are fireworks all over the sky at midnight.

Writing Practice

A. Write a Paragraph

Choose one of the topics below:

   1. Celebrating New Year
   2. Celebrating Christmas or another holiday
   3. Preparing a special dinner

B. Pre-Write

Work with a partner. Tell your partner how you celebrate the New Year (or celebrate another holiday or prepare a special dinner). Then write down what you do first, what you do next, what you do after that, and so on.

C. Outline

Number your sentences in the correct order. Then rewrite all the sentences in a paragraph. Use words showing time order. The paragraph outline below will help you.

Paragraph Outline

(Topic sentence) _____.
First, _____.
Next, _____.
Then _____.
Finally, _____.

D. Write a Rough Draft

Using the outline you made, write a rough draft of your paragraph.

E. Revise Your Rough Draft

Using the paragraph checklist below, check your rough draft or let your partner check it.

Paragraph Checklist

☐ Did you give your paragraph a title?
☐ Did you indent the first line?
☐ Did you write on every other line? (Look at pages 8 and 9 for instructions on paragraph form.)
☐ Does your paragraph have a topic sentence?
☐ Are your ideas in the correct order?
☐ Does your paragraph have a concluding sentence?

F. Edit Your Paragraph

Work with a partner or your teacher to edit your paragraph. Check spelling, punctuation, vocabulary, and grammar. Use the editing checklist below.

Editing Checklist

- ☐ Subject in every sentence?
- ☐ Verb in every sentence?
- ☐ Words in correct order?
- ☐ Sentences begin with a capital letter?
- ☐ Sentences end with a period directly at the end of a sentence?
- ☐ Sentences have a space between them?
- ☐ Commas in the correct place?
- ☐ Wrong words?
- ☐ Spelling?
- ☐ Missing words (use insertion mark: ^)?

G. Write Your Final Copy

When your rough draft has been edited, you can write the final copy of your paragraph.

Chapter

Turning Fifteen: Ceremony and Celebration

Pre-Reading

Discuss the answers to these questions with your classmates.

1. What is the older girl in the photo wearing? Why?
2. What is a special birthday for a young person in your country? What does it mean?
3. How do people usually celebrate it?

Key Vocabulary

Do you know these words? Match the words or phrases with the meanings.

1. afford ___f___
2. bouquet ___d___
3. proud of ___a___
4. pose ___e___
5. godparents ___b___
6. blessing ___c___

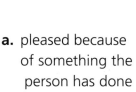

a. pleased because of something the person has done
b. adults who are close family friends and guide you through your life
c. ask for God's help and protection for someone or something
d. a bunch of flowers
e. hold yourself still for a photograph
f. have enough money for

Reading

Track 6

Turning Fifteen: Ceremony and Celebration

1   **A** *quinceañera* (pronounced "KEEN-saye-an-YEH-ra") is a special celebration held for many girls in Spanish-speaking communities of the United States and in Latin America on their 15th birthday. The celebration may be different in different countries. The word *quinceañera* can refer to the
5   celebration or to the girl. This birthday is special because it celebrates that a girl is not a child anymore and has become a woman. It is a very important day for many young girls, a day they dream about for a long time. Everyone who knows the girl will celebrate it with a church ceremony and a big party.

There is a lot of preparation before a *quinceañera* celebration. The most
10   important and expensive thing is the girl's dress. The dress is like a bride's dress but is usually pink; however, today many girls wear dresses in other light colors, also. The birthday girl chooses 14 girls and 14 boys who will be her attendants at the ceremony and the dinner dance that follows. Traditionally, these girls and boys are younger than the birthday girl, but sometimes they
15   are the same age. The dresses for the girls must be in the same color and style, just as the suits for the boys are in the same color and style. The reason for this is that all eyes will go to the birthday girl on that special day. Then the family orders a cake that is special like a wedding cake. Sometimes the **godparents** pay for it. Many times, the cake is so big that it needs a special
20   table. Next, the parents rent a hall for the party and rent a band to play music. After that, they decide on the special food to serve the guests. Often a *quinceañera* celebration can cost as much as a big wedding; the size of the party depends on how much the girl's parents can **afford**.

On the night before the girl's 15th birthday, a band plays in the evening
25   outside her window. Then the day of her birthday arrives. First, the girl's family, her godparents, and her attendants go to a religious ceremony in the church. The girl receives a **bouquet** of flowers and **blessings** and

prayers that will help her to live a strong life. Her parents are **proud of** their grown-up daughter, and they embrace her. Then she leaves the church with
her attendants and goes to the hall for the special party. Before they go to the party, they **pose** for photographs.

The hall is beautifully decorated with flowers, and it is full of guests. They wait for the girl and her family to arrive. The band plays music, and the party begins with a dinner. After the dinner, the girl dances the first dance with
her father. Then the other attendants start to dance, followed by the guests. Everyone has a good time, and they all dance until midnight. It is a day she will always remember.

Vocabulary

A. Vocabulary in Context

Complete these sentences with the following words.

afford	bouquet	pose
blessings	godparents	proud of

1. A *quinceañera* is expensive, and many parents cannot _____ to have one for their daughter.
2. The girl's _____ help her with guidance and advice throughout her life.
3. The *quinceañera* holds a _____ in the church.
4. In the church, the girl receives prayers and _____.
5. When the ceremony ends, the parents are _____ their daughter.
6. The *quinceañera* and her attendants _____ for photos to help everyone remember this special day.

Word Partnership	Use **afford** with:
v.	afford **to buy/pay, can/could** afford, **can't/couldn't** afford, afford **to lose**
adj.	**able/unable to** afford

B. Vocabulary in New Context

Answer these questions with complete sentences.

1. Who gives you guidance in your life—your godparents or someone else?

_____

2. When do you give a bouquet of flowers?

_____

3. What can you not afford to buy right now?

_____

4. What are you proud of about yourself?

_____

5. When do you pose for a photograph?

_____

6. Where can you receive a blessing?

_____

C. Vocabulary Building

Complete these sentences with the words from the box.

to dress (verb)	dress (noun)	dressy (adj.)

1. She came to the dinner in _____ clothes.
2. Girls usually like _____ for an occasion.

to differ (verb)	difference (noun)	different (adj.)

3. I asked three _____ girls and they all said the same thing.
4. She wanted her dress _____ from the others.

| to prepare (verb) | preparation (noun) | prepared (adj.) |

5. They set the already _____ dishes on the table.

6. I can't go out today because I have _____ for the test tomorrow.

Reading Comprehension

A. Looking for the Main Ideas

Circle the letter of the best answer.

1. A *quinceañera* is _____.
   a. another name for a big birthday party
   b. a 15th birthday celebration held for girls in many Latin American countries
   c. the word for "celebration" in Spanish
   d. a special birthday for boys and girls when they are 15

2. Before the *quinceañera*, _____.
   a. the girl must make a dress
   b. there is a lot of preparation
   c. the girl asks 14 boys to dance with her
   d. the girl's parents make a cake

3. On the day of the *quinceañera*, there is _____.
   a. only a church ceremony
   b. a church ceremony, a dinner, and a dance
   c. only a dinner and a dance
   d. a party for the girl's relatives

B. Looking for Details

Use complete sentences to answer the questions.

1. What is the traditional color for the *quinceañera's* dress?

_____

2. How many girl and boy attendants does she have?

_____

3. Why do the attendants wear the same color and style of clothes?

_____

4. What do her godparents give her?

_____

5. Where does she go with her attendants after the church ceremony?

_____

6. With whom does the *quinceañera* dance first?

_____

Discussion Questions

Discuss the answers to these questions with your classmates.

1. How do people celebrate a special birthday, a special day for a young person, or a name day in your country?
2. What kind of preparations do they make for this day?
3. Describe a wedding in your country.

Critical Thinking Questions

Discuss the answers to these questions with your classmates.

1. Do you think a girl becomes a woman at age 15? Why or why not? In your culture, at what age does a girl become an adult? At what age does a boy become an adult? Do you think people actually reach adulthood at different times? When do you know that a boy or girl has matured to adulthood?
2. Turning a certain age and becoming an adult is an important passage, or time of change, in life. What are some other important passages in life? Which ones have you already experienced? How did they change your life?

Writing

Writing Model

Now read the following paragraph written by a student. What country does the student come from?

A Wedding in My Country

1   Last year, my oldest brother got married. His bride was his friend's sister. First, they had a civil marriage in the town hall. A few weeks later, they had a church wedding. The bride wore a beautiful white dress and a veil over her face. The bridegroom wore a tuxedo. After the religious ceremony was over,
5   the newlyweds and the guests went to a restaurant near the church. Here there was a wonderful wedding reception with all kinds of hot and cold food. After that, there was music and dancing. Before the reception ended, the bride and groom met and thanked every guest. Finally, after the reception was over, the newlyweds went on a trip to Hawaii for their honeymoon.

Writing Skills

A. Organizing: *Review of Describing a Process*

You learned in Chapter 5 that the words below show time order:

First,. . .
Next,. . .
Then. . .
Finally/Lastly,. . .

The words **after that** also show time order. We use these words in the same way as **next** and **then**.

After that,
Next, } there was music and dancing.
Then

We use **after that, next,** and **then** at the beginning of a sentence. We cannot use them to make two sentences into a single sentence.

B. Using *before* and *after* to Show Time Order

When we describe a process, we often use dependent clauses beginning with **before** or **after**. These words show time order.

A *clause* is a group of words with a subject and a verb. There are two kinds of clauses: main clauses and dependent clauses. A *main clause* is a separate sentence. A *dependent clause* depends on the main clause; it cannot stand alone.

Exercise

1. Read each of the following clauses. If the clause is a separate sentence and can stand alone, write "main clause" under it. If the clause cannot stand alone, write "dependent clause" under it.

1. The young girl enters the church

    Example: <u>main clause</u>

2. before they eat

_____

3. after they finish the ceremony

_____

4. she invites her closest relatives

_____

5. before the church ceremony begins

_____

6. her parents embrace her

_____

7. the *quinceañera* wears a beautiful pink dress

_____

8. before they go to the party

_____

C. Writing a Dependent Clause with *before* or *after*

Look at the sentences below. Each statement has a main clause and a dependent clause.

<u>After the religious ceremony is over</u>, they go to a hall.
(dependent clause)

<u>Before they go to the party</u>, they pose for photographs.
(dependent clause)

When the dependent clause comes first, separate it from the main clause with a comma.

Exercises

2. Punctuate the following sentences with a comma where necessary.

1. Before they go to the party they pose for photographs.
2. After they have dinner there is dancing.
3. Before they have the special party they have a church ceremony.
4. After the church ceremony is over her parents embrace her.
5. Before they have a reception they must rent a hall and a band to play music.
6. After the girl and her family arrive at the hall the party can begin.

3. Use the word in parentheses to combine each pair of sentences into a single sentence. Begin with the dependent clause.

1. You have a religious ceremony. (after)
You have a dinner and dance.

Example: <u>After you have a religious ceremony, you have a dinner and dance.</u>

2. The girl and her attendants pose for photographs.
They go to the party. (before)

_____

_____

_____

3. The guests have dinner. (after)
The girl starts to dance with her father.

_____

_____

_____

4. The girl dances with her father. (after)
The other guests dance.

_____

_____

_____

4. Find the mistakes. There are 10 mistakes in grammar and punctuation. Find and correct them.

    First you need to invite your closest relatives, like parents grandparents aunts uncles godparents brothers sisters and close friends. Then, you must decide what food you will give your guests at the dinner. Next, you must pick out a church and a hall. Finally you must pick out a dress. For many girls, this is the importantest thing.

Writing Practice

A. Write a Paragraph

Choose one of the topics below:

1. A special birthday or other celebration in my country
2. A religious ceremony in my country
3. A wedding reception in my country

B. Pre-Write

Work with a partner. Tell your partner about a wedding in your country. Then write down what they do first, what comes next, what comes after that, and so on.

C. Outline

Number your sentences in the correct order. Then rewrite all the sentences in a paragraph. Use words showing time order. The paragraph outline below will help you.

Paragraph Outline

(Topic sentence) _____.
First, _____.
Next, _____.
After that,/Then _____.
After/Before _____.
Finally, _____.

D. Write a Rough Draft

Using the outline you made, write a rough draft of your paragraph.

E. Revise Your Rough Draft

Using the paragraph checklist below, check your rough draft or let your partner check it.

Paragraph Checklist

☐ Did you give your paragraph a title?
☐ Did you indent the first line?
☐ Did you write on every other line?
☐ Does your paragraph have a topic sentence?
☐ Are your ideas in the correct order?
☐ Does your paragraph have a concluding sentence?

F. Edit Your Paragraph

Work with a partner or your teacher to edit your paragraph. Check spelling, punctuation, vocabulary, and grammar. Use the editing checklist below.

Editing Checklist

- ☐ Subject in every sentence?
- ☐ Verb in every sentence?
- ☐ Words in correct order?
- ☐ Sentences begin with a capital letter?
- ☐ Sentences end with a period directly at the end of a sentence?
- ☐ Sentences have a space between them?
- ☐ Commas in the correct place?
- ☐ Wrong words?
- ☐ Spelling?
- ☐ Missing words (use insertion mark: ^)?

G. Write Your Final Copy

When your rough draft has been edited, you can write the final copy of your paragraph.

Weaving It Together

⏱ Timed Writing

Choose one of the following topics that you have not already written about in "Writing Practice." You have 50 minutes to write your paragraph.

1. A special birthday or other celebration in my country
2. A religious ceremony in my country
3. A wedding reception in my country

Connecting to the Internet

A. Use the Internet to find information about the following three festivals/holidays: Çocuk Bayrami, Kodomono-hi, and N'cwala.

Put the information in the table below.

	Çocuk Bayrami	Kodomono-hi	N'cwala
Country			
Time of Year			
What Is Celebrated			
Two Facts about How this Festival/ Holiday Is Celebrated	1. 2.	1. 2.	1. 2.

B. Use the Internet to find out about birthday celebrations in one of the following countries: Australia, China, Denmark, Ghana, or Peru. With your classmates, share your information about how birthdays are celebrated in your choice of country.

What Do You Think Now?

Refer to page 55 at the beginning of this unit. Do you know the answers now? Complete the sentence, or circle the best answer.

1. Nepal is a _____.

2. The cow is/is not important to Hindus.

3. People celebrate/don't celebrate their brothers and sisters.

4. Spanish-speaking countries have a special birthday for a girl, called a *quinceañera*, when she is _____.

5. The *quinceañera*, or special birthday, is/is not only for the girl's family.

Famous People

What Do You Think?

Answer the questions with your best guess. Circle **Yes** or **No**.

Do you think . . .

1. Braille, the reading/writing system for the blind is named after a woman? **Yes   No**
2. the blind use Braille to write in all languages? **Yes   No**
3. the blind have Braille watches? **Yes   No**
4. Hetty Green, the world's richest woman at one time, wore the same dress for years? **Yes   No**
5. Hetty Green spent a lot of money on her sick son? **Yes   No**

Chapter 7

Louis Invents Braille

Pre-Reading

Discuss the answers to these questions with your classmates.

1. What are the hands in the picture doing?
2. How can blind people read?
3. What do you know about blind people?

Key Vocabulary

Do you know these words? Match the words or phrases with the meanings.

1. infection ___e___
2. sharp ___d___
3. blind ___b___
4. tool ___a___
5. copy ___g___
6. look forward to ___c___
7. dots ___h___
8. unlucky ___f___

a. something you use for doing work
b. not able to see
c. wait with happiness for
d. able to cut easily
e. a disease you get from something or someone
f. having bad things happen by chance
g. make or do something that is the same as something else
h. small, round points

Reading

Louis Invents Braille

Track 7

1   Louis Braille was born near Paris, France, in 1809. When he was a little
boy, Louis loved to play with his father's **tools.** One day, when he was four,
he was playing with his father's tools when a **sharp** tool went into his left
eye. An **infection** started in his left eye and went to the other eye. He was
5   **unlucky.** A few weeks later, Louis was **blind.**

When Louis was 10, his parents took him to a school for blind children in
Paris. Louis lived at the school. He was a good student and **looked forward
to** the day when he could read. The school had some books that blind people
could read. These books had letters that stood out. He had to feel each letter
10 with his fingers. There was one sentence on each page. Just one part of a book
weighed 20 pounds. A whole book weighed 400 pounds! By age eleven, Louis
had read all 14 books in the school. He wanted to read more, but there were
no more books. So every evening, he tried to find a way for blind people to
be able to read books. One day, Captain Charles Barbier, a French soldier,
15 came to speak at the school. Barbier had invented night writing. This system
used **dots** for the letters of the alphabet. Soldiers could feel the dots with their
fingers and read with no light. Barbier thought night writing could also help
blind people.

Barbier's system was difficult, but it gave Louis an idea. He worked night
20 after night to make a simple system with dots. By age 15, he had finished
his system. He showed it to other students in the school, and they loved it.
They called it Braille, after him. At age 17, Louis graduated from the school
and became a teacher there. In his free time, he **copied** books into Braille.
Someone read to Louis while he made the dots. He copied the books of
25 Shakespeare and other writers into Braille. The students read all the books
and wanted more. The school did not want a 15-year-old boy's invention to
be better than their own heavy books and would not let students read Braille
books. Nevertheless, the students continued to read them. Finally, after
20 years, the school agreed to use Braille.

30　　　Louis Braille spent the rest of his life trying to tell the world about Braille. But nobody cared. Louis was unlucky again. He became very sick. Even when he was sick in his bed, he continued to write books in Braille for the students at his school. A few years later, Louis Braille died at age 43. Two years after he died, schools for the blind began to use his system.

35　　　Today, we use Braille not only to write words in all languages but also to write math and music. Blind people send Braille greeting cards, wear Braille watches, type on Braille keyboards, and take elevators with Braille controls. Louis Braille had no idea how many people he had helped. On the door of the house where he was born are the words, "He opened the doors of knowledge
40　　to all those who cannot see."

Vocabulary

A. Vocabulary in Context

Complete these sentences with the following words.

3 an infection	6 dots	1 tools
4 blind	5 looked forward to	7 unlucky
8 copied	2 sharp	

1. When Louis was a child, he played with his father's _____.

2. A _____ tool went into his eye.

3. Louis got _____ in his eye.

4. Louis became _____ when he was four years old.

5. Louis liked school and _____ the day when he could read.

6. Barbier's system used _____.

7. Louis was _____ again in life.

8. Louis _____ other books into Braille.

Word Partnership	Use **sharp** with:
n.	sharp **edge**, sharp **point**, sharp **teeth**, sharp **eyes**, sharp **mind**, sharp **criticism**, sharp **decline**, sharp **increase**, sharp **pain**, sharp **contrast**
adv.	**very** sharp

B. Vocabulary in New Context

Answer these questions with complete sentences.

1. What is the name of something sharp you use?

I use a sharp knife to cut meat

2. What day or number is unlucky for you?

The number 13 is unlucky for many cultures

3. What do you copy when you are in class?

I copy vocabulary in my class

4. What food or drink do you look forward to having when you get home?

I look forward to having a can of coke

5. What color stick does a blind person use?

A blind person use a white stick

6. Where do you put a dot when you write?

I put a dot at the end of the sentence when I write

7. What do you take when you have an infection?

I take medication when I have an infection.

8. What tool does a painter use?

A painter uses a brush and an ease

C. Vocabulary Building

Complete the sentences with the words from the box.

to infect (*verb*)	infection (*noun*)	infectious (*adj.*)

1. My little brother has an ear _____ again.
2. Our common cold is an _____ disease.

to weigh (*verb*)	weight (*noun*)	weighty (*adj.*)

3. She has a _____ decision to make today.
4. He likes _____ himself first thing in the morning.

to know (*verb*)	knowledge (*noun*)	knowledgeable (*adj.*)

5. John is very _____ about art.
6. I am amazed at her _____ of movies.

Reading Comprehension

A. Looking for the Main Ideas

Circle the letter of the best answer.

1. When Louis was four, he _____.
    a. became blind
    b. had sharp tools
    c. went to school
    d. read books

2. Charles Barbier _____.
    a. had an infection
    b. invented night writing
    c. visited soldiers
    d. became a teacher

3. By age 15, Louis _____.
    a. had died
    b. was difficult
    c. made a new system of reading
    d. had copied many books

B. Looking for Details

One word in each sentence is not correct. Rewrite the sentence with the correct word.

1. When Louis was four, a blind tool went into his eye.

_____

_____

2. Louis went to a school for unlucky children in Paris.

_____

_____

3. Barbier's system used tools for the letters of the alphabet.

_____

_____

4. Barbier thought his system could help blind people to play.

_____

_____

5. Louis died at age 34.

_____

_____

6. Today, we use Braille not only to write words in all languages but also to write art and music.

_____

_____

Discussion Questions

Discuss the answers to these questions with your classmates.

1. Do you know of other famous blind people? How are blind people special?

2. Louis Braille was unlucky. Do you know another unlucky person? Explain.

Critical Thinking Questions

Discuss the answers to these questions with your classmates.

1. Sometimes it takes many years for great inventions to become successful. What are some things that get in the way? Is it easier to get an invention to be used today than it was in Louis Braille's time? Why or why not?

2. What character traits did Louis Braille have that helped him in his life? Do you think he felt unlucky? Do you think it is more difficult for a blind or disabled person to be successful? Why or why not?

Writing

Writing Model

Now read the following paragraph written by a student.

My Sister Liz

1   My sister Liz was born lucky. She has a beautiful smile. When she does something bad, she smiles and my parents are not angry. She eats a lot and does not get fat. Her favorite meal is a double cheeseburger with french fries, a milkshake, and an ice cream sundae. She does not study hard but always
5   gets good grades. After school, she does her homework in five minutes while she watches television at the same time. In conclusion, I believe that some people are born lucky, and some are not.

Writing Skills

A. Organizing: *Unity*

As you know, a good paragraph has three parts: a topic sentence, supporting sentences, and a concluding sentence. But a good paragraph also has unity.

Unity means that all of the supporting sentences are about the controlling idea in the topic sentence. Think about the model paragraph above.

Topic sentence: My sister Liz was   <u>born lucky</u>.
                                      (controlling idea)

Main supporting sentences:

   1. She has a beautiful smile.
   2. She eats a lot and does not get fat.
   3. She does not study hard but always gets good grades.

This paragraph has unity. All the supporting sentences are about why Liz was born lucky.

B. Irrelevant Sentences

When a sentence does not belong in a paragraph, we say that it is an *irrelevant sentence.*

Example:

My sister Jamie is very shy. When there are other people around, she speaks very little. Sometimes she does not speak at all and even runs away. She is very quiet at home and at school. You do not even know she is there sometimes. She is shy about her body, too. She never goes to the beach or swimming pool. But she like ice cream and cookies.

Irrelevant sentence: But she likes ice cream and cookies.

The sentence "But she likes ice cream and cookies" does not belong in the paragraph. It does not talk about why Jamie is shy.

Exercises

1. Underline the irrelevant sentences in the following short paragraphs.

1.   George has not been lucky in school this year. He got sick and missed classes and could not take his finals. He also lost his books. These were not only his textbooks but also his notebooks. Everybody likes George because he will go out of his way to help people.

2.   My roommate Tony is very untidy. He has brown hair and blue eyes. He leaves his laundry on the floor. When he cooks, he never washes the dishes. For a while, he had a bicycle on his bed. It is not surprising that Tony can never find anything.

3.   My Uncle Conrad is very clumsy. When he drinks coffee, he always spills some on his shirt. In the shopping mall, he walks into other people all the time. He has size 14 feet. Last time he came to our house, he sat on the cat.

4. Aunt Dotty loves adventure. On her 60th birthday, she went mountain climbing in the Alps. On her 70th birthday, she went on a trip to the North Pole. When she was 80, she drove alone across the United States. She loves to eat chocolate. We all wonder what she will do when she is 90.

2. Find the mistakes. There are 10 mistakes in grammar, punctuation, and capitalization. Find and correct them.

The braille family lived in a village near paris france. There were four childrens, and Louis was the most youngest. The boy was very smart and his father hope he would grow up to be a Teacher. But then a terrible accident happened and Louis became blind.

Writing Practice

A. Write a Paragraph

Choose one of the topics below:

1. A person who is lucky or unlucky
2. A good or bad quality of a friend or family member
3. A pet cat or dog

B. Pre-Write

Work with a partner or alone.

1. Write down a topic sentence about a person or animal. You can follow this outline for a topic sentence:

What person/animal is to you	+	name	+	verb	+	adjective
My pet dog		Rex		is		very lazy.

2. List as many points as you can about the person or animal.
3. Go over each point on your list. Ask yourself, "Does this support the controlling idea?" Cross out the points that do not.

C. Outline

1. Organize your ideas. List the points in the order in which you will write about them in your paragraph.

2. Make a more detailed outline. The paragraph outline below will help you.

Paragraph Outline

(Topic sentence) _____.
(Supporting sentence 1) _____.
(Supporting detail[s]) _____.
(Supporting sentence 2) _____.
(Supporting detail[s]) _____.
(Supporting sentence 3) _____.
(Supporting detail[s]) _____.
(Concluding sentence) _____.

D. Write a Rough Draft

Using the outline you made, write a rough draft of your paragraph.

E. Revise Your Rough Draft

Using the paragraph checklist below, check your rough draft or let your partner check it.

Paragraph Checklist

- ☐ Did you give your paragraph a title?
- ☐ Did you indent the first line?
- ☐ Did you write on every other line?
- ☐ Does your paragraph have a topic sentence?
- ☐ Does your topic sentence have a controlling idea?
- ☐ Do your other sentences support your topic sentence?
- ☐ Are your ideas in the correct order?
- ☐ Does your paragraph have a concluding sentence?

F. Edit Your Paragraph

Work with a partner or your teacher to edit your paragraph. Check spelling, punctuation, vocabulary, and grammar. Use the editing checklist below.

Editing Checklist

- ☐ Subject in every sentence?
- ☐ Verb in every sentence?
- ☐ Words in correct order?
- ☐ Sentences begin with a capital letter?
- ☐ Sentences end with a period directly at the end of a sentence?
- ☐ Sentences have a space between them?
- ☐ Commas in the correct place?
- ☐ Wrong words?
- ☐ Spelling?
- ☐ Missing words (use insertion mark: ^)?

G. Write Your Final Copy

When your rough draft has been edited, you can write the final copy of your paragraph.

Chapter 8

The World's Most Unusual Millionaire

Pre-Reading

Discuss the answers to these questions with your classmates.

1. Who are some famous millionaires today?

2. What kinds of things do they own?

3. Imagine you are a millionaire. What will you spend your money on?

Check the boxes, and discuss your answers.

☐ expensive car   ☐ beautiful home   ☐ other

☐ expensive clothes   ☐ nice vacations

4. Would you give money to charity (organizations to help the sick and poor)? Why or why not?

5. The woman in the picture was a millionaire. What do you expect a millionaire to look like?

Key Vocabulary

Do you know these words? Match the words or phrases with the meanings.

1. stingy ___c___   **a.** say that you will not do or take something

2. waste ___e___   **b.** care given by doctors

3. refuse ___a___   **c.** not wanting to spend or give away money

4. raw ___f___   **d.** empty area

5. refund ___h___   **e.** not use; use when it is not necessary

6. laundry ___g___   **f.** not cooked

7. space ___d___   **g.** place where they wash and iron clothes

8. medical treatment ___b___   **h.** money you get back for something you bought

Reading

Track 8

The World's Most Unusual Millionaire

1   **H**etty Robinson was born in 1834. When her parents died, she was
30 years old. They left her $10 million ($185 million in today's dollars). She
was very good at business and soon made more money. Hetty was famous as
the richest woman in the United States, but she was also famous because she
5   was very **stingy**.

Even when she was young, she was stingy. For instance, on her 21st
birthday, she **refused** to light the candles on her birthday cake because she
did not want to **waste** them. The next day, she cleaned the candles and
returned them to the store to get a **refund**.

10   Hetty always thought men wanted to marry her for her money. Finally,
at the age of 33, she decided to get married because she did not want her
relatives to get her money. She married Edward Green, who was a millionaire.
They had a son and a daughter. Soon after, Hetty divorced him because she
did not agree with him about money matters.

15   Hetty was even stingy with her own children. For example, when her son
hurt his knee in an accident, Hetty did not call a doctor. She tried to take care
of it herself. When her son's knee didn't get better, she dressed him in old
clothes and took him to a free clinic. The doctors recognized her and asked
for money. Hetty refused to pay and took her son home. The boy did not get
20   **medical treatment**, and a few years later his leg was amputated.

Hetty was stingy with herself, too. For example, she always wore the same
black dress. As the years passed by, the color of the dress changed from black
to green and then brown. When the dress became dirty, she went to a cheap
laundry and told them to wash only the bottom where it was dirty, and she
25   waited until it was ready. Her undergarments were old newspapers she got
from the streets. She rented a cheap apartment with no heat in New Jersey
because she did not want to pay taxes in New York. Then she traveled on
the train to her office in New York. Her office was a **space** in a bank, which
the bank gave to her for free. All she ate was **raw** onions and cold oatmeal.

30 She was too stingy to spend money to heat her food. Sometimes, to heat her oatmeal, she put it on the office heater because that was free. She also ate cookies, but regular cookies were too expensive for her, so she walked a long way to get broken cookies, which were much cheaper. One time, she spent half the night looking for a two-cent stamp.

35 When Hetty Green died in 1916, she had no friends. She left more than $100 million (over $17 billion today) to her son and daughter. Her son and daughter were not stingy like Hetty, and they spent the money freely.

Vocabulary

A. Vocabulary in Context

Complete the sentences with the following words.

2 laundry	5 a refund	1 stingy
6 medical treatment	3 refused	4 waste
8 raw	7 a space	

1. Hetty did not like to spend money; she was _____.
2. Hetty went to the _____ to have the bottom part of her dress washed.
3. On her 21st birthday, Hetty _____ to light the candles on her cake.
4. Hetty liked to use everything. She did not like to _____ anything.
5. She went back to the store to get _____ of the money she paid for the birthday candles.
6. Her son hurt his knee, but he did not get _____.
7. The bank gave Hetty _____ to use as her office.
8. Hetty did not cook onions; she ate them _____.

B. Vocabulary in New Context

Work with a partner. Read the questions and add the letters to complete the answers.

1. What does a **stingy** person *not* like to spend?
   M O N E Y
2. What is the name for a green **space** in a big city?
   P ___ R ___

3. What **medical treatment** does a doctor usually give when you are sick?

    M ___ D ___ ___ ___ T ___ ___ N

4. What is something many businesspeople do *not* like to **waste?**

    _T_ _I_ M _E_

5. What is a vegetable most people do *not* eat **raw?**

    P _O_ _T_ A T _O_

Now make a sentence with each of the words in **bold**.

Example: *A stingy person does not like to spend money.*

C. Vocabulary Building

Complete the sentences with the words from the box.

to refund (verb)	refund (noun)	refundable (adj.)

1. If you are not happy with it, we will give you a _____.

2. The salesperson said that the shoes on sale are not _____.

to treat (verb)	treatment (noun)	treatable (adj.)

3. He is receiving a new _____ for his knee pain.

4. The doctor said the redness on my face was _____.

to waste (verb)	waste (noun)	wasteful (adj.)

5. My mother says it is _____ to throw away good food you don't eat.

6. I turn off the lights when I leave a room in order not _____ electricity.

Reading Comprehension

A. Looking for the Main Ideas

Circle the letter of the best answer.

1. Hetty was a very rich woman, but she was _____.
    a. stingy   c. green
    b. short   d. old

2. Hetty married _____.
   a. for love
   b. to have children

   c. so that she would not be lonely
   d. so that her relatives would not get her money

3. Hetty was even stingy with _____.
   a. Edward Green
   b. her own child

   c. her leg
   d. her parents

B. Looking for Details

Circle **T** if the answer is true. Circle **F** if the answer is false.

1. Hetty's parents died when she was 30.	**T**	F
2. Hetty ate mostly raw onions and cold oatmeal.	**T**	F
3. Hetty called the doctor for her son.	T	**F**
4. Hetty lived in New York.	T	**F**
5. Hetty lived in an apartment with no heat.	**T**	F
6. When Hetty died, she left $10 million.	T	**F**

Discussion Questions

Discuss the answers to these questions with your classmates.

1. What famous person do you know of who had a bad characteristic? Say what he or she did.

2. Describe some other types of people who are not very nice, and say why.

3. Some people are stingy about some things, but they spend money on other things. Are you this way? Give examples.

Critical Thinking Questions

Discuss the answers to these questions with your classmates.

1. Why are some of the wealthiest people stingy? Why do you think Hetty was so stingy? What events in her life might have made her that way?

2. Do you think that rich people have a moral duty to share their wealth with others who need it? Why or why not? Do you think that the wealthy countries of the world do enough to help poor countries? What are the best ways that wealthy people and countries can help others?

Exercise

1. Describe a stingy person you know. Then compare with your classmates. Who has the best example of a stingy person?

1. Identify the person.

Example: <u>Mr. Norton lives in my apartment building.</u>

_____

_____

_____

2. What does this person *not* like to spend money on (for example, food, new clothes, restaurants, gifts)?

Example: <u>This person does not like to spend money on electricity.</u>

_____

_____

_____

3. Give an example.

Example: <u>When I go to see him in his apartment in the evening, it is always dark.</u>
<u>The curtains are open so that he gets light from the street.</u>

_____

_____

_____

Writing

Writing Model

Now read the following paragraph written by a student.

My Selfish Brother

1   My brother is very selfish. He does not want to share things with other people. For example, when he buys a chocolate bar, he puts it in a secret place. Then he eats it all, by himself. He never helps anyone. He says he is busy. For example, a game of Nintendo makes him very busy. He does
5 not care if something he does bothers other people. For instance, last night he played loud rock 'n' roll music until four o'clock in the morning. In conclusion, I think my brother is selfish and will always be selfish.

Writing Skills

Organizing: *Giving Examples*

To introduce an example in your paragraph, you can use the following:

For example, . . .

or

For instance, . . .

1. Underline the words showing examples in the reading.
2. Underline the words showing examples in the model paragraph.
3. Look at the use of the comma with the words showing examples.
4. Now go back and circle all the commas with the words showing examples in the reading and in the model paragraph.

In the model paragraph, the writer used **for example** or **for instance** to give details about supporting sentences.

Topic sentence: My brother is very selfish.

Supporting sentence: He does not want to share things with other people.

Detail or example of supporting sentence: For example, when he buys a chocolate bar, he puts it in a secret place.

For example and **for instance** have the same meaning. When your sentence begins with **for example** or **for instance**, put a comma after these words.

For example, when he buys a chocolate bar, he puts it in a secret place.

or

For instance, when he buys a chocolate bar, he puts it in a secret place.

A sentence that begins with **for example** or **for instance** must be a complete sentence.

For example, Hetty Green. (*Not correct*)
For example, Hetty Green was a millionaire. (*Correct*)

Exercise

2. The following sentences are not complete or have mistakes. Write out the correct sentences.

1. For example, he gets food all over his shirt.

_____

2. For instance, she washes dishes.

_____

3. For example, she never writes down my telephone messages.

_____

4. For instance, a doctor. help people

_____

5. For instance, she always leaves the bathroom in a mess.

_____

A name of a person or a thing can follow the words **for example** and **for instance**.

Example:

Women became leaders in the last century. **For example**, Margaret Thatcher and Golda Meir were both prime ministers of their countries.

Exercises

3. Work alone, with a partner, or in a group. Think of examples for the following statements. Add more if you can.

1. There are many famous millionaires today. For example, _bill gates_ and _Warren Buffet_ are millionaires.

2. There were some famous people who were very stingy. For instance, _____ and _____ were stingy.

3. Some people in history did very bad things. For example, _____ and _____ did terrible things.

4. Write a complete sentence as an example for each statement. Use **for instance** or **for example** in the correct form.

1. My grandfather is very forgetful.

For instance, he always forgets to tie shoes

_____

2. My English teacher has an excellent memory.

For example, she always remembers every student by

name

3. My sister is not an electrician, but she can fix many electrical things in the house.

For example, she can fix our computers

_____

5. Find the mistakes. There are 10 mistakes in grammar, punctuation, capitalization, and spelling. Find and correct them.

Howard hughes was born in texas in 1906. He was one of the richest men in the world but he was very strange. For example he eats the same dinner every night: a steak a potato and 12 peas. Later in his life, he became even stranger. For instance: he did not wear clothes and did not cut his hare. Hughes dies without any friends in 1976.

Writing Practice

A. Write a Paragraph

Choose one of the topics below:

1. A stingy person I know
2. A person who has a bad characteristic (for example, selfish, inconsiderate, lazy, etc.)
3. An unusual person

B. Pre-Write

Work with a partner or alone.

1. Write down a topic sentence about a person. (Choose from the topics above.)
2. List as many points as you can about the person.
3. Go over each point on your list. Ask yourself, "Does this support the controlling idea?" Cross out the points that do not.
4. Think of an example for each point. If you cannot find an example, cross out the point.

C. Outline

1. Organize your ideas. List the points in the order in which you will write about them in your paragraph. You should have two or three points.
2. Make a more detailed outline. The paragraph outline on the next page will help you.

Paragraph Outline

(Topic sentence) _____.

(Supporting sentence 1) <u>For example,</u> _____

_____.

(Supporting sentence 2) <u>For instance,</u> _____

_____.

(Supporting sentence 3) <u>For example,</u> _____

_____.

(Concluding sentence) _____.

D. Write a Rough Draft

Using the outline you made, write a rough draft of your paragraph.

E. Revise Your Rough Draft

Using the paragraph checklist below, check your rough draft or let your partner check it.

Paragraph Checklist

- ☐ Did you give your paragraph a title?
- ☐ Did you indent the first line?
- ☐ Did you write on every other line?
- ☐ Does your paragraph have a topic sentence?
- ☐ Does your topic sentence have a controlling idea?
- ☐ Do your other sentences support your topic sentence?
- ☐ Are your ideas in the correct order?
- ☐ Do you have examples?
- ☐ Does your paragraph have a concluding sentence?

F. Edit Your Paragraph

Work with a partner or your teacher to edit your paragraph. Check spelling, punctuation, vocabulary, and grammar. Use the editing checklist below.

Editing Checklist

- ☐ Subject in every sentence?
- ☐ Verb in every sentence?
- ☐ Words in correct order?
- ☐ Sentences begin with a capital letter?
- ☐ Sentences end with a period directly at the end of a sentence?
- ☐ Sentences have a space between them?
- ☐ Commas in the correct place?
- ☐ Wrong words?
- ☐ Spelling?
- ☐ Missing words (use insertion mark: ^)?

G. Write Your Final Copy

When your rough draft has been edited, you can write the final copy of your paragraph.

Weaving It Together

⏱ Timed Writing

Choose one of the following topics that you have not already written about in "Writing Practice." You have 50 minutes to write your paragraph.

1. A stingy person I know
2. A person who has a bad characteristic (for example, selfish, inconsiderate, lazy, etc.)
3. An unusual person

Connecting to the Internet

A. Use the Internet to find information about the following famous blind people of the past and present: Helen Keller, Stevie Wonder, Francesco Landini, Andrea Bocelli, and Esref Armagan. Find out when and where they were born and why they are or were famous.

B. Who are some of the richest people in the world? Use the Internet to find the world's 10 richest people. Then look up the following wealthy people: Oprah Winfrey, Bill Gates, and Ratan Tata. Find out how each of these people got their money, how and where they live, and how they use their money to help others.

What Do You Think Now?

Refer to page 81 at the beginning of this unit. Do you know the answers now? Complete the sentence, or circle the best answer.

1. Braille, the reading/writing system for the blind is named after (a man/woman).
2. The blind use _____ to write in all languages.
3. The blind (have/don't have) Braille watches.
4. Hetty Green, the world's richest woman at one time, (did/did not) wear the same dress for years.
5. Hetty Green (spent/did not spend) a lot of money on her sick son.

Nature Attacks!

What Do You Think?

Answer the questions with your best guess. Circle **Yes** or **No**.

Do you think . . .

1. more men die from lightning than women?	**Yes**	**No**
2. you must go under a tall tree when there is lightning?	**Yes**	**No**
3. killer bees started in Africa?	**Yes**	**No**
4. five bee stings can kill a person?	**Yes**	**No**
5. it is easy to tell a killer bee from a normal bee?	**Yes**	**No**

Chapter

9 A Dangerous Light

Pre-Reading

Discuss the answers to these questions with your classmates.

1. What is happening in the picture?
2. How can lightning be dangerous?
3. What can you do to protect against a lightning strike?

Key Vocabulary

Do you know these words? Match the words or phrases with the meanings.

1. lightning bolt __b__
2. amaze __g__
3. injured __d__
4. explode __e__
5. protect __c__
6. attract __a__
7. shelter __f__
8. frighten __h__

a. make someone or something want to come there
b. bright flash of light you see in the sky during a storm
c. stop someone or something from being harmed
d. hurt
e. blow apart, like a bomb
f. building or place where you are safe from harm
g. surprise greatly
h. make afraid

Reading

Lightning

Track 9

1 **E**very second of every day, all over the world, there are more than 100 **lightning bolts.** That's about ten million lightning bolts in one day! Lightning **amazes** us, but it can also **frighten** us. We have good reason to be afraid of lightning. Every year, about 100 people in the United States and
5 Canada die from lightning, and another 300 are **injured.** It is strange that of all the people who die from lightning, 84 percent are men. Lightning is the main cause of forest fires; it starts more than 9,000 fires each year.

Lightning is electricity inside a cloud. Scientists do not know exactly what makes this electricity. But they know that the electricity inside a cloud
10 can be as much as 100 million volts. From this extremely strong electricity, a lightning bolt, like a streak of bright light, comes down from the sky. Its temperature can reach 50,000 degrees Fahrenheit within a few millionths of a second. That's almost five times the temperature on the sun's surface. The lightning bolt is very quick. It can move at a speed of 87,000 miles per second.
15 A rocket traveling at this speed would reach the moon in 2.5 seconds. With the lightning bolt, we usually hear thunder, which is the sound of hot air **exploding.** Lightning and thunder happen at exactly the same time, but we see lightning first because light travels a million times faster than sound.

Lightning often strikes tall buildings. However, many buildings have
20 lightning rods to **protect** them from lightning. When lightning strikes, the electricity goes safely down the metal rod to the ground. Benjamin Franklin, the American statesman, invented the lightning rod in 1760. That is why buildings like the Empire State Building in New York City are safe. Lightning may hit this building as many as 12 times in 20 minutes and as often as 500
25 times a year. Airplanes are not as easy to protect as buildings, and accidents do happen. In 1963, a Boeing 707 jet was hit by lightning and crashed. Eighty-one people died.

If you see thunder and lightning coming, here are some things you can do to protect yourself. Go inside a house, get into a car, or go under

30 a bridge. If you cannot find **shelter,** go to the lowest point on the ground. If you are outside, remember that trees **attract** lightning, especially tall trees. Never go under a tall tree that stands alone. If you are in a field, drop to your knees, bend forward, and put your hands on your knees. Do not lie down because the wet ground can carry lightning. Stay

35 away from a lake, an ocean, or any other water. Don't touch or go near anything metal, such as a metal fence, golf clubs, and bicycles, because metal attracts lightning very quickly. Don't use a telephone except in an emergency.

They say that lightning never hits the same place twice, but this is not

40 true. One man, Roy Sullivan, was hit by lightning seven different times in his life. He was injured each time but did not die. He died in 1983, but not from lightning. He killed himself because he loved a woman, but she didn't love him!

Vocabulary

A. Vocabulary in Context

Complete these sentences with the following words.

2 amaze	frightened	8 protects
attract	4 injured	7 shelter
5 exploding	1 lightning bolts	

1. There are millions of _____ every day.
2. A sky with lightning can _____ you.
3. Many people are _____ when they see lightning because it is dangerous.
4. When lightning strikes people, they can be _____ or die.
5. Thunder sounds as if fireworks are _____.
6. A lightning rod _____ buildings from lightning strikes.
7. In a storm, you should find _____ from the bad weather.
8. Tall buildings _____ lightning strikes.

B. Vocabulary in New Context

Answer the questions with complete sentences.

1. What is something you can wear or carry that protects you from the rain?

I carry an umbrella to protect myself from rain

2. What kind of weather situation frightens you?

Tornado frightens me

3. What modern invention amazes you?

Computers amaze me.

4. You are in the country, and it starts to rain. Where can you go for shelter?

you can go into your car as a shelter during rainy weather.

5. What is something that can explode?

A bomb can explode

6. In what situation can a person be injured?

A person can be injured in a car accident

7. What kind of place attracts you for a vacation?

C. Vocabulary Building

Complete these sentences with the words from the box.

to amaze (*verb*)	amazement (*noun*)	amazing (*adj.*)

1. What an _____ story!

2. He looked at us in _____.

to frighten (*verb*)	fright (*noun*)	frightening (*adj.*)

3. I had a _____ when I saw him unexpectedly.

4. We had a _____ experience on the plane.

to attract (*verb*)	attraction (*noun*)	attractive (*adj.*)

5. There's an _____ woman at the party.

6. The castle is the main _____ of the city.

Reading Comprehension

A. Looking for the Main Ideas

Circle the letter of the best answer.

1. Lightning _____.
   a. is not dangerous
   b. kills only men
   c. kills and injures many people
   d. happens about 100 times a day

2. Lightning _____.
   a. and thunder happen at the same time
   b. is as hot as the surface of the sun
   c. comes after thunder
   d. is hot air exploding

3. Lightning often strikes _____.
   a. Americans
   b. tall men
   c. tall buildings
   d. New York City

B. Looking for Details

Use complete sentences to answer the questions.

1. How many people die from lightning in the United States and Canada every year?

_____

_____

2. Why do we see lightning before we hear thunder?

_____

_____

3. Why is it not a good idea to touch metal when there's lightning?

_____

_____

4. Which building in New York City gets hit by lightning 500 times a year?

_____

_____

5. Who invented the lightning rod?

_____

_____

6. How did Roy Sullivan die?

_____

_____

Discussion Questions

Discuss the answers to these questions with your classmates.

1. Why do you think more men than women die from lightning?
2. Almost every day, there is a natural disaster in the news. It could be a hurricane, a snowstorm, a flood, or an earthquake. What makes you most afraid?
3. The disasters that we are most likely to remember are those that happen closest to where we live. Can you remember a disaster (fire, plane crash, etc.) that happened near where you live? Tell about it.

Critical Thinking Questions

Discuss the answers to these questions with your classmates.

1. What is the worst weather that your country has? What must people do to protect themselves during this kind of weather? What is the best weather that your country has? Should people not live in certain places because of the weather? Why or why not?
2. Do you think Roy Sullivan was a lucky man or an unlucky man? Explain.

Writing

Writing Model

Now read the following paragraph written by a student.

A Frightening Experience

1   October 1, 1987, was a terrifying day for me. It was 7:30 on a Thursday
morning in Mexico. I was alone because my parents were out of town.
Suddenly, the room started to shake. Some dishes fell to the floor. I did not
know what to do, so I got under a table. A few minutes later, I came out and
5   tried to turn on the television, but the electricity was off. After that, I tried
the telephone, but it did not work. Shortly after, the neighbors came to see
if I was all right. Finally, at about 9:00 a.m., the telephone rang. It was my
mother. She was calling from Mexico City. She was more frightened than
I was.

Writing Skills

A. Organizing: *A Narrative Paragraph*

The paragraph you just read is a *narrative paragraph*. A narrative paragraph
tells a story about something that happened. In a narrative paragraph, you must
use a good time order for your sentences. This means that the sentences must be
in the order in which the story happened.

Exercise

1. The following sentences are about a terrifying day, but they are not in the
correct time order. Number them in the correct order.

   a. _____ I got under the table.
   b. _____ I came out and tried the telephone, but it did
   not work.

c. _____ Shortly after that, the neighbors came to see if I was all right.

d. _____ The room started to shake.

B. Words Showing Time Order

The next step is to add words that show time order to connect your sentences. These words show the order in which things happened in time.

October 1, 1987, . . .
At 9:00 A.M., . . .
Suddenly, . . .
A few minutes later, . . .
After that, . . .
Shortly after, . . .
Finally, . . .

Exercise

2. Now underline the words showing time order in the model paragraph.

C. Punctuation: *The Comma (,) with Time and Place Expressions*

Look at the words showing time order. Look at the use of the comma after words showing time order. Now go back to the model paragraph and circle all the commas after the words showing time order.

We also use a comma with dates and place names.

Dates

We use a comma to separate a date from a year:

I came to the United States on March 4, 2006.
They were married on July 26, 2008.

We use a comma after the year when a sentence continues:

October 1, 1987, was the day of the earthquake.
On March 27, 1964, a big earthquake hit Alaska.

Place Names

We use a comma to separate a city from a state or a city from a country:

> We were at home in Anchorage, Alaska.
> I come from Tokyo, Japan.

We use a comma after a state or country when the sentence continues:

> Crescent City, California, is on the coast.

Exercises

3. Put a comma where necessary in the following sentences.

1. The San Francisco earthquake hit on the morning of April 8, 1906.
2. On November 26 2004 a tsunami hit Asia.
3. The tsunami hit Telewatta Sri Lanka.
4. The biggest earthquake recorded in North America was the earthquake on March 27, 1964.
5. Suddenly, people heard a noise like thunder.
6. An earthquake hit southern Sumatra on September 12, 2007.
7. A terrible earthquake hit Kobe, Japan, in 1995.
8. Tsunamis hit Sumatra, Indonesia after this.
9. A few minutes later buildings washed away.
10. Shortly after, tsunamis hit the coast of Sri Lanka.

4. Find the mistakes. There are 10 mistakes in punctuation and capitalization. Find and correct them.

   In the United States, the States with the greatest number of deaths from lightning are Florida texas and north Carolina. Avoid these states, especially in June, which is the worst month for lightning. The other bad months are august, july april and September.

Writing Practice

A. Write a Narrative Paragraph

Choose one of the topics below:

1. A frightening experience
2. A dangerous experience
3. A strange experience

B. Pre-Write

Work with a partner or alone. Tell your partner about your experience. Then write answers to the questions below.

1. When and where did the experience occur?

_____

_____

2. What happened first?

_____

_____

3. What happened after that?

_____

_____

4. What happened at the end?

_____

_____

C. Outline

Write the sentences in the order in which they happened. Then use the words showing time order. The paragraph outline below will help you.

Paragraph Outline

(Date) was a _____ day for me. I was _____
because _____.
Suddenly, _____.
A few minutes later, _____.
Shortly after that, _____.
Finally, _____.

D. Write a Rough Draft

Using the outline you made, write a rough draft of your paragraph.

E. Revise Your Rough Draft

Using the paragraph checklist below, check your rough draft or let your partner check it.

Paragraph Checklist

- ☐ Did you give your paragraph a title?
- ☐ Did you indent the first line?
- ☐ Did you write on every other line?
- ☐ Does your paragraph have a topic sentence?
- ☐ Does your topic sentence have a controlling idea?
- ☐ Do your other sentences support your topic sentence?
- ☐ Are your ideas in the correct order?
- ☐ Does your paragraph have a concluding sentence?

F. Edit Your Paragraph

Work with a partner or your teacher to edit your paragraph. Check spelling, punctuation, vocabulary, and grammar. Use the editing checklist on the next page.

Editing Checklist

☐ Subject in every sentence?
☐ Verb in every sentence?
☐ Words in correct order?
☐ Sentences begin with a capital letter?
☐ Sentences end with a period directly at the end of a sentence?
☐ Sentences have a space between them?
☐ Commas in the correct place?
☐ Wrong words?
☐ Spelling?
☐ Missing words (use insertion mark: ^)?

G. Write Your Final Copy

When your rough draft has been edited, you can write the final copy of your paragraph.

Chapter

10 Killer Bees on the Attack

Pre-Reading

Discuss the answers to these questions with your classmates.

1. How are bees useful to people?
2. Are you afraid of bees? Why or why not?
3. When do bees sting a person?

Key Vocabulary

Do you know these words? Match the words or phrases with the meanings.

1. breed ___b___   a. move toward violently
2. attack ___a___   b. produce young
3. spread ___d___   c. get away
4. escape ___c___   d. cover a larger area
5. tell the difference ___f___   e. bright; filled with light
6. shiny ___e___   f. know one thing from another

Reading

Killer Bees on the Attack

Track 10

1   Killer bees started in Brazil in 1957. A scientist in São Paulo wanted bees to make more honey, so he put 46 African bees in with some Brazilian bees. The bees started to **breed** and make a new kind of bee. However, the new bees were a mistake. They did not want to make more honey; they wanted 5 to **attack**. Then, by accident, 26 African bees **escaped** and bred with the Brazilian bees outside.

    Scientists could not control the problem. The bees **spread**. They went from Brazil to Venezuela and then to Central America. Now they are in North America. They travel about 390 miles a year. Each group of bees, or colony, 10 grows to four times its old size in a year. This means that there will be one million new colonies in five years.

    Killer bees are very dangerous, and people are right to be afraid of them. When killer bees attack people, they attack in great numbers and often seriously hurt or kill people. Four hundred bee stings can kill a person. A total of 15 8,000 bee stings is not unusual for a killer bee attack. In fact, a student in Costa Rica had 10,000 stings and died. Often, the bees attack for no reason. They may attack because of a strong smell that is good or bad or because a person is wearing a dark color, has dark hair, or is wearing some kind of **shiny** jewelry.

    What can you do if you see killer bees coming toward you? The first thing 20 you can do is run—as fast as you can. Killer bees do not move very fast, but they will follow you up to one mile. Then you must go into the nearest house or tent. Do not jump into water. The bees will wait for you to come out of the water. Killer bees will try to attack the head or the face, so cover your head with a handkerchief or a coat. You may even take off your shirt and cover 25 your head. Stings to your chest and back are not as dangerous as stings to your head and face. However, if the bees sting you many times, you must get medical attention immediately.

    How are killer bees different from normal honey bees? Killer bees are a little smaller than regular bees, but only an expert can **tell the difference**. Killer

30 bees get angry more easily and attack more often than honey bees. Killer bees attack and sting in great numbers. Like honey bees, each killer bee can sting only one time, and the female bee dies after it stings. Killer bees also make honey, but a honey bee makes five times more honey than a killer bee.

Up to now, killer bees have killed about 1,000 people and over 100,000 cows 35 in the Americas. In the United States alone, five people have died from killer bee stings since 1990. The first American died from bee stings in Texas in 1993. From Texas, the bees moved to Nevada, New Mexico, Arizona, and then Southern California. Where will they go next?

Vocabulary

A. Vocabulary in Context

Complete the sentences with the following words.

2 attack	3 escaped	5 spread
4 breed	6 shiny	1 tell the difference

1. It is not easy to _____ between a honey bee and a killer bee because they look almost the same.
2. Killer bees _____ people and animals for no reason.
3. Twenty-six African bees _____ outside.
4. The African bees and the Brazilian bees started to _____ and make a new kind of bee.
5. The new bees went from one country to another. They _____ quickly.
6. Killer bees attack people who are wearing _____ objects like jewelry.

Word Partnership	Use **escape** with:
n.	**chance to** escape, escape **from prison**
v.	**make an** escape, **try to** escape, **manage to** escape

B. Vocabulary in New Context

Answer the questions with complete sentences.

1. What animal breeds quickly?

Rabbits breed quickly

2. What dangerous animal may attack people?

Lions may attack people.

3. What disease spreads easily?

The flu can spreads easily

4. What kinds of animals are dangerous if they escape?

Lions are dangerous when they escape.

5. What shiny pieces of jewelry do people wear?

People wear bracelets and shiny earrings.

6. How can you tell the difference between a glass cup and a plastic cup?

We can tell the difference between glass cup and plastic cup by weighting it

C. Vocabulary Building

Complete these sentences with the words from the box.

to die (verb)	death (noun)	deadly (adj.)

1. He lived in New York until his _____.
2. The blowfish has a _____ poison.

to move (verb)	movement (noun)	moving (adj.)

3. It is a very _____ film.
4. There was no _____ in the area where the noise came from.

to mean (verb)	meaning (noun)	meaningful (adj.)

5

6

5. I don't understand the _____ of this word.

6. He gave her a _____ gift.

Reading Comprehension

A. Looking for the Main Ideas

Circle the letter of the best answer.

1. A scientist wanted bees _____.
   a. to go to Africa
   b. to make more honey
   c. to attack
   d. to breed more

2. Scientists _____.
   a. could not control the problem
   b. went to Brazil
   c. grew every year
   d. traveled to North America

3. People are afraid of killer bees because they _____.
   a. sting
   b. attack and sting in large groups
   c. attack and die
   d. follow you

B. Looking for Details

Answer the questions with complete sentences.

1. Where did the killer bees go after they left Central America?

_____ North America _____

2. What colors do killer bees like to attack?

_____ dark color _____

3. What part of the body do killer bees try to attack?

_____ head or face _____

4. How many times does each killer bee sting?

_____

5. When did the first American die from killer bees?

_____

6. How many people have died from killer bees up to now?

_____

Discussion Questions

Discuss the answers to these questions with your classmates.

1. Have you been stung by a bee? What happened?
2. What is a good thing to do when a bee stings you?
3. What insects do you have in your country? Are these insects a problem?
4. What other insects or animals are you afraid of?

Critical Thinking Questions

Discuss the answers to these questions with your classmates.

1. What are some of the most dangerous animals in your country and in the world? Do you think humans should live among dangerous animals? Why or why not? What do you think of the people who try?
2. Killer bees are not natural. They are a scientific mistake. Do you think scientists should be allowed to experiment with animals and plants? What good has come from experiments with animals and plants? What bad has happened?
3. Since the early days of ships and travel, people have brought plants and animals to other countries from one part of the world to another. What good has this done? What problems has it caused?

Writing

Writing Model

Now read the following paragraph written by a student.

Cockroaches *con gián*

1   Cockroaches have become a major problem in our building, for several reasons. First, cockroaches (or roaches) carry germs and disease. Because roaches inhabit areas where there is food, we may get sick from the food we eat. Second, roaches eat everything. They eat not only food but also glue,
5   paint, clothes, wallpaper, and even plastic. There is a feeling of horror and disgust because everything in our home is destroyed by roaches. They even live in and eat the television set. Finally, roaches are indestructible. Nothing can kill the roaches in our building. All the chemical powders and sprays we have tried on them are no good. They always come back. It is either them or
10 us, so we have decided to move out.

Writing Skills

Organizing: *Giving Reasons*

In this lesson, you will learn how to *give reasons* for a situation. Usually, there is more than one reason for a situation. It is important to look at all the reasons. When there are many reasons, there is usually one that is most important.

When you write your reasons, remember the following:

1. Think of or discuss all the reasons. There is probably more than one.
2. Support your reasons. Give examples.
3. State your most important reason last. This will make your paragraph more interesting. If you give your most important reason first, the reader may not feel it necessary to read the rest of your paragraph.

Transitions for Giving Reasons: *Because*

Because answers the question "Why?" **Because** comes before the part of the sentence that gives the reason. The reason can come before or after the statement.

Examples:

Statement: We may get sick from the food we eat.

Reason: Roaches inhabit areas where there is food.

We may get sick from the food we eat **because** roaches inhabit areas where there is food.

or

Because roaches inhabit areas where there is food, we may get sick from the food we eat.

Note: Use a comma after the reason if you start the sentence with **because**.

Exercises

1. Join the sentences with **because**. Write each sentence in two ways. First, use **because** in the middle. Then use **because** in the beginning.

1. There is a feeling of disgust. Everything in our home is destroyed by roaches.

_____

_____

2. We are going to move out. The roaches are not moving out.

_____

_____

3. Nothing can kill roaches. Roaches are indestructible.

_____

_____

4. People are afraid of the killer bees. The bees attack more often than a normal bee.

_____

_____

5. The killer bees are spreading. Scientists cannot control them.

_____

_____

2. Find the mistakes. There are 10 mistakes in grammar, punctuation, and capitalization. Find and correct them.

A man from texas died after he had been stung forty times as he was trying to remove a nest. Since january 1 2000, there has been two serious attacks in las vegas. Bees stung a 79-year-old man thirty times, but he lived. In march bees covered a 77-year-old woman who is walking down the street. The bees were attracted to something she was carrying in her bag. Firefighters covered the woman with water to remove more than 200 bees from her. Bees sting the woman more than 500 times, but she lived.

Writing Practice

A. Write a Paragraph

Choose one of the topics below:

1. An animal or insect I dislike
2. An animal or insect that is a problem
3. A disease that is a problem

B. Pre-Write

Work with a partner or alone.

1. Write your topic at the top of your paper.
2. Then think of as many reasons about the topic as you can. Write every word or phrase that comes into your mind about the topic. Write down as much information as you can.

3. Write your ideas in any order you like. Do not worry about whether or not the idea is important. Write it down.

C. Outline

1. Organize your ideas.

Step 1: Write the main idea sentence.

Step 2: Pick the best reasons from the ones you wrote.

Step 3: Order your reasons. Don't forget to put your most important reason last.

Step 4: Remember to use these transitions for giving reasons:

The first reason is . . .	or	First, . . .
The second reason is . . .	or	Second, . . .
The final reason is . . .	or	Finally, . . .

2. Make a more detailed outline. The paragraph outline below will help you.

Paragraph Outline

                    for several reasons.

(Supporting fact)   The first reason is _____

(Supporting fact)   The second reason is _____

(Supporting fact)   The final reason is _____

(Concluding sentence) _____

D. Write a Rough Draft

Using the outline you made, write a rough draft of your paragraph.

E. Revise Your Rough Draft

Using the paragraph checklist on the next page; check your rough draft or let your partner check it.

Paragraph Checklist

- ☐ Did you give your paragraph a title?
- ☐ Did you indent the first line?
- ☐ Did you write on every other line?
- ☐ Does your paragraph have a topic sentence?
- ☐ Does your topic sentence have a controlling idea?
- ☐ Do your other sentences support your topic sentence?
- ☐ Are your ideas in the correct order?
- ☐ Does your paragraph have a concluding sentence?

F. Edit Your Paragraph

Work with a partner or your teacher to edit your paragraph. Check spelling, punctuation, vocabulary, and grammar. Use the editing checklist below.

Editing Checklist

- ☐ Subject in every sentence?
- ☐ Verb in every sentence?
- ☐ Words in correct order?
- ☐ Sentences begin with a capital letter?
- ☐ Sentences end with a period directly at the end of a sentence?
- ☐ Sentences have a space between them?
- ☐ Commas in the correct place?
- ☐ Wrong words?
- ☐ Spelling?
- ☐ Missing words (use insertion mark: ^)?

G. Write Your Final Copy

When your rough draft has been edited, you can write the final copy of your paragraph.

Weaving It Together

⏱ Timed Writing

Choose one of the following topics that you have not already written about in "Writing Practice." You have 50 minutes to write your paragraph.

1. An animal or insect I dislike
2. An animal or insect that is a problem
3. A disease that is a problem

Connecting to the Internet

A. The Internet contains useful information on how to prepare for a natural disaster. Find out how to prepare for one of these disasters: earthquake, flood, hurricane, tornado, or volcano eruption. Make a short list of **5** important things to do. Add the name of the Website that gave you the best information.

B. Use the Internet to find the answers to any **3** of the following questions:
• What should you do if ants invade your house?
• What should you do if you see a snake in your house?
• What should you do if you see termites?
• What should you do if you see cockroaches everywhere?
• What should you do if a dog attacks you?

What Do You Think Now?

Refer to page 107 at the beginning of this unit. Do you know the answers now? Complete the sentence, or circle the best answer.

1. More men (die/don't die) from lightning than women.
2. You (must/must not) go under a tall tree when there is lightning.
3. Killer bees started in _____.
4. _____ bee stings can kill a person.
5. It (is/is not) easy to tell a killer bee from a normal bee.

Inventions

What Do You Think?

Answer the questions with your best guess. Circle **Yes** or **No**.

Do you think . . .

1. the inventors of Yahoo! were three students?	**Yes**	**No**
2. Yahoo! Mail is the world's largest e-mail service?	**Yes**	**No**
3. *yahoo* is a Japanese word?	**Yes**	**No**
4. humans sometimes use a sheep's heart for heart transplants?	**Yes**	**No**
5. scientists can change all living cells?	**Yes**	**No**

Chapter
11 A Yahoo! Is Born

Pre-Reading

Discuss the answers to these questions with your classmates.

1. For what do you most often use a computer?
2. Do you use Yahoo! to search the Web? If not, what do you use?
3. How often do you e-mail your friends? Do you know what a blog is? Do you blog? Can you go a day without e-mailing or blogging?

Key Vocabulary

Do you know these words? Match the words or phrases with the meanings.

1. categories ___d___
2. communicate ___a___
3. keep track of ___e___
4. on campus ___f___
5. play (around) ___g___ with
6. rough ___h___
7. trailer ___c___
8. Websites ___b___
9. manners ___i___

a. exchange information with other people
b. places on the Internet where you can find information
c. a home you pull behind a car or truck
d. groups of things or people with the same qualities
e. to know where things are when there are a lot of things
f. on the land where a college or school is
g. try something in different ways to find the best way
h. not gentle or polite
i. behavior; a way of acting

Reading

A Yahoo! Is Born

Track 11

1   The year was 1994. David Filo and Jerry Yang were both students at Stanford University in California. They were studying engineering and lived in a **trailer on campus**. David and Jerry were like most students. They loved to work on their favorite hobby. But their hobby was very different

5   from others. It became a billion-dollar company! It changed the way people **communicate** with each other, find information, and buy products on the Internet.

David and Jerry didn't always like to study. One day they were both bored, so they decided to **play around with** the Internet. They found some

10 good **Websites**. But there was so much information on the Internet! So they developed a way to find and **keep track of** all their favorite Websites. First they had long lists of Websites. Later on, they separated them into **categories**. Even these started to become big again, so they separated the categories into more groups. In the beginning, they called their new system

15 "Jerry and David's Guide to the World Wide Web."

Later, David and Jerry changed the name of "Jerry and David's Guide to the World Wide Web" to "Yahoo!" They liked the word because it means someone who is rude, **rough**, and without good **manners**. They thought it was funny. They put their Yahoo! on two student computers. Part of it went

20 on Jerry's computer, "Akebono." The other part went on David's computer, "Konishiki." They were the names of two famous sumo wrestlers.

After a while, students, friends, and others started to use Yahoo!, and they loved it. Soon, hundreds of people outside Stanford University's campus were using it. They told other students and friends about it. In a short time,

25 thousands of people were using it. By the autumn of 1994, almost 100,000 people were using this great new invention.

David and Jerry were working 20 hours a day, but they didn't care. They had fun and loved what they were doing. But as Yahoo! became more and more popular, David and Jerry became serious about their product. They felt

30   they were offering a service people really wanted. They began to realize that
       this was something special and could be a great business.

           David and Jerry got all the papers necessary to have their own company.
       Then they went to other people and businesses and asked them for money to
       start their new company. Finally, a business called Sequoia Capital gave them
35   almost two million dollars.

           David and Jerry believed in their idea. They hired some people to help
       them. The company grew quickly. Today, hundreds of millions of people
       around the world use Yahoo! There are Yahoo! offices in Europe, Asia, Latin
       America, Australia, Canada, and the United States. Over 12,000 people are
40   working for Yahoo! worldwide. The main offices are in Sunnyvale, California.

           Yahoo! still helps people find information, but the company does many
       other things too. It offers many Internet services such as e-mail, instant
       messaging, Websites, blogging, advertising, and other business uses. Today,
       Yahoo! Mail is the largest e-mail service in the world. Yahoo! has its products
45   in over 20 languages around the world. That's a long way from a hobby in a
       student trailer. Think about how many times you have used Yahoo!

Vocabulary

A. Vocabulary in Context

Complete these sentences with the following words.

2 categories   8 manners   8 rough
1 communicate   play around with   4 trailer
7 keep track of   3 on campus   6 Websites

1. The creation of Yahoo! changed the way people _____ with each
other, find information, and buy things on the Internet.

2. David and Jerry separated their long list of Websites into _____.

3. David and Jerry lived on the grounds of Stanford University. They lived

_____.

4. They didn't live in an apartment. They lived in a _____.

5. They didn't like to study, so they started to _____ the Internet.

6. David and Jerry found a lot of good _____ on the Internet.

7. David and Jerry found so many Websites on the Internet that it was hard to
_____ them all.

8. The meaning of Yahoo! is someone who is _____ and without good _____.

Word Partnership	Use **manner** with:
adj. effective manner, **efficient** manner, **abrasive** manner, **abrupt** manner, **appropriate** manner, **businesslike** manner, **different** manner, **friendly** manner, **usual** manner	

B. Vocabulary in New Context

Answer the questions with complete sentences.

1. What is your favorite Website?

My favorite website is facebook

2. What is your favorite way of communicating with friends?

My favorite way of communicating with friends is chating

3. What do you do to keep track of time when you are on the Internet?

When I'm on the internet, I'am keeping track of time by looking at the time on the computer.

4. What is the name of a building you see on campus?

I see a cafteria on campus

5. How many Websites do you usually play around with before you buy something on the Internet?

C. Vocabulary Building

Complete these sentences with the words from the box.

| to believe (verb) | belief (noun) | believable (adj.) |

1. His excuse was _____.
2. We found his story hard _____.

| to develop (verb) | development (noun) | developing (adj.) |

3. Computers are a rapidly _____ industry.
4. The company is spending billions on _____.

| to communicate (verb) | communication (noun) | communicative (adj.) |

5. _____ exercises are important in language learning.
6. There was no _____ between us.

Reading Comprehension

A. Looking for the Main Ideas

Circle the letter of the best answer.

1. David and Jerry's hobby was different from others because _____.
   a. it helped them find information
   b. they lived in a trailer on campus
   c. they were university students
   d. it became a huge and important company

2. David and Jerry's invention started out as a way to _____.
   a. make long lists
   b. play around with the Internet
   c. keep track of their favorite Websites
   d. avoid studying for their classes

3. David and Jerry started Yahoo! _____.
   a. with their own money
   b. even though they weren't serious about their invention
   c. with help from another business
   d. before anyone knew about their idea

B. Looking for Details

Answer the questions with complete sentences.

1. What did David and Jerry first develop when they were playing around with the Internet?
2. What did David and Jerry first call their new system?
3. Why did David and Jerry like the word *yahoo*?
4. By the autumn of 1994, how many people were using David and Jerry's new system?
5. After Yahoo! became more popular, what did David and Jerry begin to realize?
6. What service does Yahoo! provide today that is the largest in the world?

Discussion Questions

Discuss the answers to these questions with your classmates.

1. Why do people invent things?
2. What is your favorite invention? Why is it useful?
3. Make a list of some inventions you use.

Critical Thinking Questions

Discuss the answers to these questions with your classmates.

1. Yahoo! provides such services as e-mail, instant messaging, and blogging. What are the advantages of these services? What are the disadvantages?
2. How does the Internet affect people's lives around the world? How has it changed what people know and the way they do things?

Writing

Writing Model

Read the following paragraph written by a student.

My New Cell Phone

1   I got a new cell phone for my birthday, and I soon realized what a useful invention this is. I travel a lot, so someone can get in touch with me wherever I am. If I am busy when the phone rings, they can leave a message and I can call back. It doesn't matter where I am. Sometimes when I am traveling,
5   I see something I want to remember. Now I can take a photo of it because my new cell phone has a camera in it. Therefore, I do not need to take a camera with me. It is also so small and light, so it is easy to carry in your pocket. In conclusion, I really do not know how I lived without this wonderful invention.

Writing Skills

A. Organizing: *Cause-and-Effect Paragraph*

In Unit 5 we looked at the word **because**, which introduces the reason for or cause of something. In this lesson, we will look at the effect of something.

First, you must see the difference between the *cause* and the *effect*. The following examples show the cause and the effect. Notice that an effect can have several causes.

Examples:

Mary was late for work. **(effect)**
She said her alarm clock does not work. **(cause)**

This machine does not work. **(effect)**
It is not plugged in. **(cause)**

There are no computers in our school. **(effect)**
The school does not have money to buy them. **(cause)**
There is no room to put them in the school. **(cause)**
Most of our teachers do not like computers. **(cause)**

Exercise

1. Say which statement is the cause and which is the effect.

1.	This light is out.	*effect*
2.	There is no light bulb.	*cause*
3.	The telephone does not work.	e
4.	The storm last night pulled the lines down.	c
5.	I forgot to put batteries in it.	c
6.	My portable radio does not work.	e
7.	The flight from Canada is three hours late.	e
8.	There is a snowstorm in Canada.	c
9.	I cannot see well with these old glasses.	e
10.	I need to have my eyes tested again.	c
11.	The printer needs a new cartridge.	c
12.	There is no writing when I print out.	e

B. Using *so* and *therefore*

Look at the model paragraph. Underline the words **so** and **therefore.** Both of these words introduce effect clauses. Now look at the punctuation used with these words. Circle the punctuation before and after these words.

Example:

$$\text{I am not disturbed} \begin{cases} \text{, so} \\ \text{; therefore,} \\ \text{. Therefore,} \end{cases} \text{I can do more work.}$$

So and **therefore** have the same meaning, but **therefore** is more formal.

Exercises

2. Punctuate these sentences with a comma where necessary.

1. Mr. Jones has a hearing problem; therefore, he wears a hearing aid.
2. Janet does not like to wear her glasses, so she is wearing contact lenses.
3. Peter bought an expensive car. Therefore, he had to get a car alarm.
4. John got a photocopier for his office, so he does not have to rush to the copy store every day.
5. Kathy always has her cell phone with her; therefore, you can contact her at any time.
6. Tony hates to wash dishes, so he bought a dishwasher.

3. Choose the best clause from the list below to complete each sentence.

4 I am not home during the day
2 My alarm clock does not work
5 Typing is not so important for most office jobs today
1 His phone is out of order
6 I studied in the language lab all last semester
3 My eyesight is not so good in the dark

1. _____ ;

therefore, there is a busy signal on his phone all the time.

2. _____ ,

so I got up late.

3. _____ .

Therefore, I drive very carefully at night.

4. _____ ,

so I leave my answering machine on.

5. _____ ;

therefore, I am learning to use a computer.

6. _____ .

Therefore, my English pronunciation is much better.

4. Find the mistakes. There are 10 mistakes in grammar and capitalization. Find and correct them.

Two other student from Stanford University california starting a project on 1996. They created a search engine. They called them Google. It becomes very populars. People started to use the verb *to google* when he wanted to look up something in the Internet. Today, the verb *google* is in the Dictionary.

Writing Practice

A. Write a Paragraph

Choose one of the topics below:

1. A great invention (microwave, World Wide Web, etc.)
2. An object that I want to invent
3. An invention that I don't like

B. Pre-Write

Work with a group, a partner, or alone.

1. Write your topic at the top of your paper.
2. Think of as many causes and effects about the topic as you can.
3. Write down every word or phrase that comes into your mind about the topic.
4. Write your ideas in any order you like. Don't worry about whether or not the idea is important. Write it down.

C. Outline

1. Organize your ideas.

Step 1: Write the main idea sentence.

Step 2: Pick three of the best causes and effects from the ones you wrote.

Step 3: Remember to use the words **so** and **therefore.**

2. Make a more detailed outline. The paragraph outline below will help you.

Paragraph Outline

(Topic sentence)	_____.
(Cause 1)	_____,
(Effect)	so _____.
(Cause 2)	_____.
(Effect)	Therefore, _____.
(Cause 3)	_____;
(Effect)	_____.
(Concluding sentence)	Therefore, _____.

D. Write a Rough Draft

Using the outline you made, write a rough draft of your paragraph.

E. Revise Your Rough Draft

Using the paragraph checklist on the next page, check your rough draft or let your partner check it.

Paragraph Checklist

☐ Did you give your paragraph a title?
☐ Did you indent the first line?
☐ Did you write on every other line?
☐ Does your paragraph have a topic sentence?
☐ Does your topic sentence have a controlling idea?
☐ Do your other sentences support your topic sentence?
☐ Are your ideas in the correct order?
☐ Does your paragraph have a concluding sentence?

F. Edit Your Paragraph

Work with a partner or your teacher to edit your paragraph. Check spelling, punctuation, vocabulary, and grammar. Use the editing checklist below.

Editing Checklist

☐ Subject in every sentence?
☐ Verb in every sentence?
☐ Words in correct order?
☐ Sentences begin with a capital letter?
☐ Sentences end with a period directly at the end of a sentence?
☐ Sentences have a space between them?
☐ Commas in the correct place?
☐ Wrong words?
☐ Spelling?
☐ Missing words (use insertion mark: ^)?

G. Write Your Final Copy

When your rough draft has been edited, you can write the final copy of your paragraph.

Chapter
12 Biotechnology: Changing Living Things

Pre-Reading

Discuss the answers to these questions
with your classmates.

1. What is unusual about the plants and animals in the photos?
2. Do you think these plants and animals are natural? Where
   do you think they come from?
3. What are some plants and animals that humans have created?

Key Vocabulary

Do you know these words? Match the words or phrases with the meanings.

1. breed ___h___   **a.** plants grown for food
2. cell ___c___   **b.** to come away from the surface
3. crops ___a___   **c.** the smallest part of an animal or plant
4. genes ___g___   **d.** not harmed by
5. insecticides ___f___   **e.** covered with; enveloped by
6. peel/peel off ___b___   **f.** chemicals used to kill insects
7. resistant ___d___   **g.** part of a cell which controls physical characteristics
8. wrapped ___e___   **h.** produce animals with certain qualities

Reading

🔊 Biotechnology: Changing Living Things

1   **P**eople use biotechnology to change living things. Biotechnology creates new animals, plants, foods, medicines, and materials. People have used biotechnology for thousands of years. They have created new plants, animals, and microbes[1] that make cheese, yogurt, bread, beer, and wine. Biotechnology

5   advanced very quickly when DNA was discovered in 1953. Every living **cell** has DNA. DNA is made up of **genes**. Today, scientists who work in biotechnology can change genes and change living cells.

   Farmers have been changing the genes of **crops** like corn, wheat, and rice for thousands of years, and today we grow better and better crops. As the

10   world population is increasing, we need more and more food. In the 1960s, food scientists made new kinds of crops like corn, wheat, and rice. These crops grew faster, bigger, and were more **resistant** to disease. For example, in 1992 an American company changed the genes in some cotton plants. The change made the leaves poisonous to certain kinds of insects that eat cotton plants,

15   but nothing else. In this way, farmers grow more crops and do not need to use harmful **insecticides**.

   Our fruits and vegetables are also changing. When we go to the supermarket today, we may see many kinds of tomatoes. They have different colors and sizes. Some tomatoes are long-life types, meaning they stay fresh

20   longer. They are red and have a perfect shape, but they don't get soft. These tomatoes have had their genes changed. We do not know if changing the genes of plants we eat will be good for our health. Likewise, we do not know what will happen to other natural plants that grow near these plants.

   People have bred animals for thousands of years and have created

25   different breeds of domestic animals. For example, we **breed** horses for horse racing and cows that give more milk. Scientists have sped up the process in the last 20 years. They have created animals that are useful to humans. In

---

[1]**microbe:** a very small living cell that can be seen only with a microscope

1994, scientists in Australia invented a way of removing the wool from sheep without cutting it off. They gave the sheep a special hormone[2] and **wrapped** a hairnet[3] around them. After three weeks, they could **peel off** the wool by hand. Scientists have used pigs to help humans receive heart transplants. Pigs and humans have different genes. However, the heart of a pig is similar to the human heart in size and shape. Scientists put human genes into pigs. This makes it possible for the human body to accept the heart of a pig in a transplant operation.

Scientists are also using biotechnology to clean up dangerous places. When oil from ships or factories spills into the sea, it is poisonous. The poisons endanger plants and animals in the area. The poisons can also be passed on to the food we eat. Certain microbes can break up the oil. In laboratories, scientists now grow microbes that can digest or break up the oil. In 1999, scientists in the United States developed a new microbe that eats waste material at nuclear sites and makes the sites less harmful. Sometimes there is too much arsenic, a poison, in the ground. A little arsenic is fine, but too much is dangerous to plants, animals, and people. Scientists have now created a plant that sucks up the arsenic from the ground.

There are more bio-inventions, and there will be many more bio-inventions in the future to help all of us in different ways. But will they be good or bad for us?

---

[2]**hormone:** a chemical in the body
[3]**hairnet:** a fine net with elastic on the edges that one wears over his or her hair to
keep it in place

Vocabulary

A. Vocabulary in Context

Complete these sentences with the following words.

breed	genes	resistant
cell	insecticides	wrapped
crops	peel off	

1. We grow _____ like corn, wheat, and rice for food.

2. In 1994, in Australia, they _____ a hairnet around a sheep.

3. Today, some Australians don't have to cut the wool off sheep. They can _____ the wool by hand.
4. Every _____ has DNA.
5. The _____ in cells tell us the characteristics of the living thing.
6. Farmers used harmful _____ to kill insects on crops.
7. Farmers want to _____ cows that give more milk.
8. Insects don't eat some crops, because these crops are _____ to them.

B. Vocabulary in New Context

Answer the questions with complete sentences.

1. What is a breed of animal that you like?
2. What is a crop that grows in your country?
3. What is a fruit whose skin you peel off before you eat it?
4. What is something that you get that is wrapped?
5. Whose genes do you have? (your father's/mother's)
6. When do people use insecticides in the home or garden?

C. Vocabulary Building

Complete these sentences with the words from the box.

to resist (*verb*)	resistance (*noun*)	resistant (*adj.*)

1. He was very _____ to the idea of moving.
2. He has a strong _____ to catching colds.

to peel (*verb*)	peel (*noun*)	peeling (*adj.*)

3. I slipped on a banana _____ this morning.
4. Do you want me _____ the orange?

to operate (*verb*)	operation (*noun*)	operational (*adj.*)

5. The system will be _____ by the end of the year.
6. The surgeon decided _____ on his patient's kidney.

Reading Comprehension

A. Looking for the Main Ideas

Circle the letter of the best answer.

1. Because of biotechnology, we have _____.
   a. a larger world population
   b. less need for food
   c. more harmful insecticides
   d. better crops

2. Scientists today use biotechnology to _____.
   a. make animals more like humans
   b. create animals that are more useful to humans
   c. make farm animals less important
   d. study breeders that lived thousands of years ago

3. Scientists grow microbes that can _____.
   a. make more oil
   b. suck up arsenic from the ground
   c. create nuclear material
   d. clean up dangerous materials

B. Looking for Details

Circle **T** if the sentence is true. Circle **F** if the sentence is false.

1. People learned to use microbes to make cheese, yogurt, and bread. **T**   F
2. Even with biotechnology, scientists cannot change living cells.   T   **F**
3. Scientists made crops like corn and rice that grew faster and bigger. **T**   F
4. We do not know if changing plant genes will be good for our health.   **T**   F
5. Scientists in Australia invented a way to take wool without killing sheep.   T   **F**
6. Any arsenic in the ground is not good.   T   **F**

Discussion Questions

Discuss the answers to these questions with your classmates.

1. If you could change a plant or animal in some way (for example, make broccoli that tastes like chocolate or a bee that doesn't sting), what would you do?
2. For thousands of years, farmers planted the seeds from the best plants. They also learned how to grow two plants together to make a new plant. What are some of the reasons why people wanted to change plants? What are some reasons why people wanted to change animals?

Critical Thinking Questions

Discuss the answers to these questions with your classmates.

1. Race horses have long, thin legs that break easily. Some dogs have such flat faces that they cannot breathe right. Why do breeders make animals that have certain traits that might harm them? Do you think this is wrong? Some people want to stop breeders from changing animals in ways that will harm them. Do you agree with this idea?
2. With biotechnology, scientists are now able to make clones (identical copies) of sheep, dogs, and many other types of animals. Do you think this is right? What is good about cloning? What is bad about it? Do you think there should be laws against human cloning? Why or why not?

Writing

Writing Model

Read the following paragraph written by a student.

Biotechnology for Our Food

1   In my opinion, we get some advantages if we use biotechnology for our food. First of all, it will help to have more food for everybody. The new crops grow faster and bigger. Second, the new crops do not need insecticides. This will be better for our health because insecticides are harmful. In addition, we
5   will have better fruits and vegetables. Today, we have watermelon and grapes with no seeds. These are better than watermelon and grapes with seeds. In conclusion, biotechnology for our food will give us more food, the food will be better for our health, and we will have better fruits and vegetables.

Writing Skills

A. Organizing: *Advantages and Disadvantages*

The paragraph above tells us the advantages (the good sides) of something. It is organized in this way. First is the topic sentence. Then comes the advantage, starting with

> **First of all, . . .**
>
>> or
>
> **First, . . .**
>
>> or
>
> **The first advantage is . . .**

and followed by a supporting sentence.

Then comes the next advantage, starting with

Second, . . .

or

The second advantage is . . .

and followed by a supporting sentence.

Any other advantages also start with

In addition, . . .

or

Moreover, . . .

and are followed by a supporting sentence.

At the end is

In conclusion, . . .

Read the model paragraph again. How many advantages are there?

B. Fact or Opinion?

Now look at the topic sentence of the model paragraph. The student gives us a statement of opinion. It is not a fact. A statement of fact gives information that everyone thinks is true. An opinion tells us what one person thinks is true. Other people may have different opinions.

If your statement is an opinion, you can start with one of the following:

In my opinion, . . .
I believe . . .
I think . . .
I feel . . .

After you give an opinion, you must support it with facts and/or examples.

Exercise

1. Are the statements below facts or opinions? Circle the correct answer.

   1. Biotechnology is one of the best ways to solve the problem of world hunger.

     Fact   Opinion ✓

   2. Biotechnology helps keep our environment clean.

     Fact ✓   Opinion

   3. In 1992, an American company changed the genes in cotton plants.

     Fact ✓   Opinion

   4. Today, scientists grow microbes that can break up oil.

     Fact ✓   Opinion

   5. There will be many more wonderful bio-inventions in years to come.

     Fact   Opinion ✓

C. Transitions Showing Addition: *in addition* and *moreover*

When you give a list of advantages, reasons, or other ideas in a paragraph, you can use transitions that show addition. Transitions like **in addition** and **moreover** show addition. **In addition** and **moreover** have the same meaning.

     First (of all), . . .
     Second, . . .
     In addition, . . .
     Moreover, . . .
     Finally, . . .

   In addition and **moreover** are not always placed at the beginning of the sentence.

   Look at the examples below and note the punctuation used with each.

Examples:

   In addition, we will have better fruits and vegetables.

   We will have, **in addition,** better fruits and vegetables.

   Moreover, we will have better fruits and vegetables.

   We will have, **moreover,** better fruits and vegetables.

Now underline the transition that shows addition in the model paragraph. Circle the punctuation marks before and after the transition words.

Exercises

2. In the sentences below, **in addition** and **moreover** are used in the middle of sentences. Rewrite the sentences. Put the words **in addition** and **moreover** at the beginning of the sentences. Use the correct punctuation.

1. Biotechnology creates new animals, plants, and foods. Biotechnology, in addition, provides us with new medicines and materials.

_____

_____

2. Scientists in the 1960s made corn, wheat, and rice that grew faster and bigger. Scientists, moreover, made these crops more resistant to disease and insects.

_____

_____

3. Today, American farmers can grow more crops. American farmers, in addition, do not need to use so many insecticides.

_____

_____

4. Tomatoes that have had their genes changed are red and have a perfect shape. These tomatoes, moreover, stay fresh longer.

_____

_____

5. Scientists have created cattle that have more meat. Scientists, in addition, have created pigs that help people with heart transplants.

_____

_____

6. Using biotechnology, scientists have created microbes that can break up oil. Scientists, moreover, have created a plant that takes arsenic from the ground.

_____

_____

3. Find the mistakes. There are 10 mistakes in grammar, punctuation, and capitalization. Find and correct them.

China is a large country with many people to feed. In the future, China will. needs even more food. In the past, the chinese government does not allow plants that had their genes changed. Today, however chinese scientists are work hard to change the genes of rice. They want to create rice that grows in cold temperatures, high, places, and dry soil. In addition, they want rice that has much vitamins and resists insects.

Writing Practice

A. Write a Paragraph

Choose one of the topics below:

1. The disadvantages of biotechnology for our food
2. The advantages or disadvantages of biotechnology for animals
3. The advantages or disadvantages of biotechnology for humans

B. Pre-Write

Work with a group, a partner, or alone.

1. Write your topic at the top of your paper.
2. Think of as many reasons to support your opinion as possible. Remember to choose only one side: advantages or disadvantages.
3. Which of these reasons can you support with facts or examples?

C. Outline

1. Organize your ideas.

    Step 1: Write the topic sentence, which tells the reader your position on the subject (Advantages/Disadvantages of . . .). If it is an opinion, use the words "In my opinion, . . ." or "I believe . . ." or something similar.

    Step 2: Pick three supporting reasons for your opinion. Make sure that these reasons are different from each other and that you can write a supporting sentence (with a fact or personal example) for each.

    Step 3: Remember to introduce each reason.

2. Make a more detailed outline. The paragraph outline below will help you.

Paragraph Outline

(Topic sentence)   _____.
(First advantage/disadvantage)   _____.
(Supporting sentence)   _____.
(Second advantage/disadvantage)   _____.
(Supporting sentence)   _____.
(Third advantage/disadvantage)   _____.
(Supporting sentence)   _____.
(Concluding sentence)   _____.

D. Write a Rough Draft

Using the outline you made, write a rough draft of your paragraph.

E. Revise Your Rough Draft

Using the paragraph checklist on the next page, check your rough draft or let your partner check it.

Paragraph Checklist

- ☐ Did you give your paragraph a title?
- ☐ Did you indent the first line?
- ☐ Did you write on every other line?
- ☐ Does your paragraph have a topic sentence?
- ☐ Does your topic sentence have a controlling idea?
- ☐ Do your other sentences support your topic sentence?
- ☐ Are your ideas in the correct order?
- ☐ Does your paragraph have a concluding sentence?

F. Edit Your Paragraph

Work with a partner or your teacher to edit your paragraph. Check spelling, punctuation, vocabulary, and grammar. Use the editing checklist below.

Editing Checklist

- ☐ Subject in every sentence?
- ☐ Verb in every sentence?
- ☐ Words in correct order?
- ☐ Sentences begin with a capital letter?
- ☐ Sentences end with a period directly at the end of a sentence?
- ☐ Sentences have a space between them?
- ☐ Commas in the correct place?
- ☐ Wrong words?
- ☐ Spelling?
- ☐ Missing words (use insertion mark: ^)?

G. Write Your Final Copy

When your rough draft has been edited, you can write the final copy of your paragraph.

Weaving It Together

⏱ Timed Writing

Choose one of the following topics that you have not already written about in "Writing Practice." You have 50 minutes to write your paragraph.

1. The disadvantages of biotechnology for our food
2. The advantages or disadvantages of biotechnology for animals
3. The advantages or disadvantages of biotechnology for humans

Connecting to the Internet

A. Use the Internet to look up the early history of Apple or Microsoft. Answer the following questions:
   - Who started the company?
   - Where and when did the company start?
   - What was the company the first to do?

B. Use the Internet to find out the advantages and disadvantages of crops made with biotechnology. Fill in the chart.

| Crops Made with Biotechnology ||
Advantages	Disadvantages

What Do You Think Now?

Refer to page 133 at the beginning of this unit. Do you know the answers now? Complete the sentence, or circle the best answer.

1. The inventors of Yahoo! were _____ students.
2. Yahoo! Mail (is/isn't) the world's largest e-mail service.
3. *Yahoo* (is/isn't) a Japanese word.
4. Humans sometimes use a _____ heart for heart transplants.
5. Scientists (can/cannot) change all living cells.

Customs and Traditions

What Do You Think?

Answer the questions with your best guess. Circle **Yes** or **No**.

Do you think . . .

1. brides wear white all over the world?   **Yes**   **No**
2. many Chinese couples see a fortune teller for a suitable wedding day?   **Yes**   **No**
3. in the English-speaking world, Brown is the most common last name?   **Yes**   **No**
4. many people in the U.S., England, Australia, and Vietnam have middle names?   **Yes**   **No**
5. in the U.S. you can change your name to a famous person's name?   **Yes**   **No**

Chapter

13 Flowers, Dishes, and Dresses

Pre-Reading

Discuss the answers to these questions with your classmates.

1. In your country, what traditions take place before a wedding?
2. What do brides and grooms wear on their wedding day?
3. What do people give the bride and groom for good luck?

Key Vocabulary

Do you know these words? Match the words with the meanings.

1. charms _____
2. bride _____
3. groom _____
4. informal _____
5. aisle _____
6. crown _____
7. symbolize _____
8. faithfulness _____

a. represent; mean
b. walkway in a supermarket or church
c. a circle made of gold or jewels that a king or queen wears on the head
d. not official; relaxed and friendly
e. a woman who is getting married
f. truthfulness
g. a man who is getting married
h. objects that have magic powers

Reading

Flowers, Dishes, and Dresses

Track 13

1　　**W**edding traditions are different from culture to culture. Most people follow the traditions of their culture and usually do not know what the traditions mean. In the past, friends and relatives of the newlyweds wanted them to be happy and have good fortune or luck. This was the start of

5　　traditions to bring good luck to the couple and the use of good-luck **charms**. Many of these traditions still continue today.

　　To make sure the wedding goes well and the couple will have good fortune, many people around the world follow the old traditions. In Germany, before the wedding day, friends and family of the **bride** and **groom** bring old dishes.

10　　They throw the dishes on the floor. The dishes break in front of the bride and groom, who then must clean them up. The people all have fun doing this and have an **informal** party. This tradition prepares the couple for married life and brings them good luck. Similarly, at an English wedding, church bells ring when the bride enters the church and walks up the **aisle**. Sometimes there

15　　are flower petals where the bride walks. Likewise, in some countries, there are flower petals on the marriage bed to wish the couple happiness in the future.

　　The date of the wedding day can be important for a couple's good fortune too. There are many traditions about wedding dates. In China the couple may see a fortune teller, who will find a favorable day based on the dates when

20　　the couple was born. In the United States today, no special day or month is favorable for weddings. However, June is a popular month. The month of June is named after the Roman goddess Juno. She is the goddess of love and marriage. On the other hand, in some countries, the day of the week is important. For example, in Italy a wedding is usually on a Sunday, but in the

25　　United States it is usually on a Saturday.

　　Many countries around the world use good-luck charms for good fortune or luck for the bride and to make bad spirits go away. On the wedding day in the United States, brides wear white dresses. Some brides follow the old tradition of wearing "Something old, something new, something borrowed,

30　　something blue." Each "something" has a special meaning. "Something old"

symbolizes a connection to the bride's family and the past. "Something new" symbolizes the success and good fortune in the bride's new life. For "something borrowed," the bride borrows something from a friend or family member and then returns it after the wedding. This symbolizes love and
35   support of family and friends. "Something blue" is because the color blue stands for **faithfulness**. Likewise, in Norway, a bride wears a white dress. However, some brides may wear a traditional crown. The **crown** is silver and has charms hanging from it. When the bride walks, the charms make a beautiful sound. The sound is to tell bad spirits to go away. Similarly, in
40   Sweden, there is an old tradition for good luck that some people still follow. The mother of the bride gives her daughter a gold coin for her right shoe. The father of the bride gives her a silver coin for her left shoe. The bride wears the coins in her shoes on her wedding day. In this way, the parents hope she will never be poor. Brides usually wear white in the West; however, in some Asian
45   countries, brides wear red. Red is the color of happiness, good luck, and life. At a Chinese wedding, the bride usually wears a red dress, and sometimes all candles and decorations for the wedding are red too. Similarly, an Indian bride wears a red *sari*,[1] which symbolizes life and energy.

    In conclusion, there are many different wedding traditions around the
50   world. Most traditions come from long ago, when people believed in the power of charms and ceremonies to bring good luck and keep bad luck away. Similarly, people today want to celebrate the newlyweds and wish them good fortune and happiness in their new lives.

----

[1]**sari:** a dress which is worn by Indian women and made of one long piece material that is wrapped around the body

Vocabulary

A. Vocabulary in Context

Complete these sentences with the following words.

aisle	crown	informal
bride	faithfulness	symbolize
charms	groom	

1. In a church, the bride walks down the _____.

2. In most western countries, the _____ usually wears white.

3. In most western countries, the _____ usually wears a dark suit.

4. Some brides in the United States follow the old tradition and wear _____ for good luck.

5. In Norway, some brides wear a traditional _____ on the head.

6. In India, brides wear red to _____ life and energy.

7. In Germany, some couples have an _____ party before the wedding.

8. The color blue represents _____ in the United States.

B. Vocabulary in New Context

Answer the questions with complete sentences.

1. Who wears a crown today?

_____

_____

2. What color dress does a bride in your country wear?

_____

_____

3. What is a lucky charm in your country?

_____

_____

4. What does the color white symbolize in your country?

_____

_____

5. What kind of clothes would you wear for an informal party?

_____

_____

6. What does a groom wear for his wedding in your country?

_____

_____

C. Vocabulary Building

Complete these sentences with the words from the box.

to symbolize (*verb*)	symbol (*noun*)	symbolic (*adj.*)

1. He is a _____ of freedom for his people.

2. The wedding ring has a _____ meaning. Do you know what it is?

to charm (*verb*)	charm (*noun*)	charming (*adj.*)

3. He knows how _____ the ladies.

4. That's a _____ house!

to marry (*verb*)	marriage (*noun*)	married/marriageable (*adj.*)

5. June is a popular month _____ in the United States.

6. The _____ will take place at 2 o'clock.

Reading Comprehension

A. Looking for the Main Ideas

Circle the letter of the best answer.

1. In Germany, the tradition of breaking dishes is supposed to _____.
   a. show the couple that friends and family support them
   b. bring the couple money in the future
   c. allow the couple to share their feelings before the marriage
   d. prepare the couple for their life together

2. In many countries, the date of the wedding is _____.
   a. set by the bride's parents
   b. important for the couple's good fortune
   c. not part of the old wedding traditions
   d. decided by a fortune teller

3. Wedding traditions are _____.
   a. almost the same around the world
   b. a way for relatives and friends to enjoy themselves
   c. meant for celebrating the couple and bringing them luck
   d. a way to make the bride and groom wealthy

B. Looking for Details

Circle **T** if the sentence is true. Circle **F** if the sentence is false.

1. In China, a fortune teller sometimes sets the wedding date based on the couple's birth dates.   **T**   **F**
2. The month of June is named after Juno, the goddess of good fortune.   **T**   **F**
3. Many brides wear blue dresses in the United States.   **T**   **F**
4. "Something borrowed" symbolizes the love and support of family and friends.   **T**   **F**
5. The charms on a crown are a symbol of faithfulness.   **T**   **F**
6. In many Asian countries, red is the color of happiness and good luck.   **T**   **F**

Discussion Questions

Discuss the answers to these questions with your classmates.

1. What ceremonies and rituals take place during a wedding in your country? What do they mean? Where do they come from?
2. What good-luck charms do people use, carry, or wear in your country? Do you believe in good-luck charms? Do you believe there is good luck and bad luck in people's lives? Why or why not?
3. What type of wedding would you like for yourself? Do you prefer a large, traditional wedding?

Critical Thinking Questions

Discuss the answers to these questions with your classmates.

1. Why do people follow traditions, even in modern society? Why are these traditions important? What would life be like without any traditions?
2. Do you think that wedding traditions and good-luck charms can bring happiness to a marriage? Why or why not? What makes a marriage happy and long lasting?
3. Do your parents and grandparents follow more traditions than you do? How is your life similar to and different from theirs? How do you think the lives of the next generation will be alike and different from yours?

Writing

Writing Model

Now read the following paragraph written by a student.

Wedding Customs

1   There are some similarities and differences in wedding customs between North America and my country. First, the couple wears special wedding clothes. In North America, the bride wears a white dress and usually a veil. The groom wears a dark suit or a tuxedo. Similarly, in my country, the
5   bride wears a white dress and a veil. However, the groom does not wear a tuxedo. He wears a dark suit. Next, there is a wedding reception after the religious wedding. In North America, the reception can be a sit-down meal or appetizers. Likewise, in my country the reception is a sit-down meal. However, in my country there is more food on the tables. Also, the wedding
10 reception in North America ends by a certain time such as midnight. However, in my country, the reception continues until the morning. In conclusion, there are both similarities and differences in the wedding customs between my country and North America.

Writing Skills

A. Organizing: *Comparing and Contrasting*

In this unit, you will learn how to organize a compare-and-contrast paragraph.
When we *compare*, we look at the similarities between two things, two people, two ideas, and so on. When we *contrast*, we look at the differences.
There are two ways of organizing your paragraph when you compare and contrast. Plan A and Plan B are outlines of the two ways you can organize your compare-and-contrast paragraph.

Look at the outlines, and then look at the model paragraph just given. Which outline does it follow—Plan A or Plan B? How many similarities can you see in the model paragraph? How many differences can you see in the model paragraph?

Plan A

Topic sentence
  I. Similarities: North America and my country
    A. The wedding clothes
    B. The wedding reception
 II. Differences: North America and my country
    A. The wedding clothes
    B. The wedding reception
Concluding sentence

Plan B

Topic sentence
  I. The wedding clothes
    A. Similarities: North America and my country
    B. Differences: North America and my country
 II. The wedding reception
    A. Similarities: North America and my country
    B. Differences: North America and my country
Concluding sentence

B. Transitions Showing Contrast: *however*

However connects an idea in the first sentence with a contrasting idea in the second sentence. **However** tells the reader that an idea opposite from the one in the first sentence will follow. **However** has the same meaning as **but. However** is used mostly in formal writing. Notice the punctuation used with **however**. Both of the following examples have the same meaning.

Examples:

In the United States, there is no special month that is favorable; **however,** June is a popular month for weddings.

In the United States, there is no special month that is favorable. **However,** June is a popular month for weddings.

Now underline the transition **however** in the reading passage and in the model paragraph. Next, look at the punctuation with **however**. Go back and circle all the punctuation marks with **however**.

Exercise

1. Connect the following sentence with however. Use **however** with both kinds of punctuation.

    1. The Hindu bride wears red clothes. A Japanese bride wears white.

    _____

    _____

    2. Some brides in England wear a penny in their shoe. In Sweden, the bride puts a gold coin in her right shoe and a silver coin in her left.

    _____

    _____

    3. In Finland, it is traditional for a bride to wear a crown. In the United States, the bride usually wears a veil.

    _____

    _____

    4. In Turkey, if you catch a candy that the bride throws, you will wed soon. In America, you will marry soon if you catch the bride's bouquet.

    _____

    _____

C. Transitions Showing Similarity: *similarly* and *likewise*

The transitions **similarly** and **likewise** connect an idea in the first sentence with a similar idea in the second sentence. **Similarly** or **likewise** introduces the second sentence. Use a comma after **similarly** or **likewise**.

Example:

In Brazil, a bridegroom can't see the bride in her wedding dress before the ceremony. In Spain, the groom must not see the bride's dress or the bride will have bad luck.

In Brazil, a bridegroom can't see the bride in her wedding dress before the ceremony. **Similarly,** / **Likewise,** } in Spain, the groom must not see the bride's dress or the bride will have bad luck.

Exercises

2. Connect the following sentences with **similarly** or **likewise**. Use the correct punctuation.

1. In Nepal, red powder on a woman's forehead shows that she is married. An American woman wears a ring on her left hand.

_____

_____

2. In India, some marriages are arranged. In Afghanistan, fathers often arrange their sons' and daughters' marriages.

_____

_____

3. In China, friends and guests play jokes on the couple. In Saudi Arabia, a groom's friends often play jokes on him.

_____

_____

4. In France, the newlyweds drink wine from a traditional wedding cup. In Japan, a couple drinks rice wine from a small cup.

_____

_____

3. Find the mistakes. There are 10 mistakes in grammar, punctuation, and capitalization. Find and correct them.

Many countries have a wedding cake tradition. The bride and groom together cut a pieces of the wedding cake. the groom feeds the cake to the bride. Then the bride feed the cake to the groom. Everyone claps and cheered. This traditions of the cake is symbolic. It symbolize that the couple have started to take care of each other. However at some wedding today, the bride and groom put the cake in each others face!

Writing Practice

A. Write a Paragraph

Choose one of the topics below to compare and contrast:

1. Wedding customs in your country and in North America (or another country)
2. Past and present wedding customs (any country)
3. Wedding receptions for the wealthy and not so wealthy (any country)

B. Pre-Write

Work with a group, a partner, or alone.

1. Write your topic at the top of your paper.
2. Think of as many similarities as you can. Write them down.
3. Think of as many differences as you can. Write them down.

C. Outline

1. Organize your ideas.

   Step 1: Write your topic sentence.

Example:

There are some interesting similarities and differences in wedding customs between North America and my country, _____.

Step 2: Name two things that make them similar. Then name two things that make them different.

Step 3: Can you write at least one supporting sentence for each of the similarities and differences above? If you can't find good examples, you may have to change your points.

Step 4: Remember the compare-and-contrast transitions: **however, likewise** and **similarly**. Think of where you can put these in your paragraph.

2. Make a more detailed outline. The paragraph outline below will help you.

Paragraph Outline

(Topic sentence) _____.

(Similarity 1) _____.

(Supporting sentence) _____.

(Similarity 2) _____.

(Supporting sentence) _____.

(Difference 1) _____.

(Supporting sentence) _____.

(Difference 2) _____.

(Supporting sentence) _____.

(Concluding sentence) _____.

D. Write a Rough Draft

Using the outline you made, write a rough draft of your paragraph.

E. Revise Your Rough Draft

Using the paragraph checklist below, check your rough draft or let your partner check it.

Paragraph Checklist

☐ Did you give your paragraph a title?
☐ Did you indent the first line?
☐ Did you write on every other line?
☐ Does your paragraph have a topic sentence?
☐ Does your topic sentence have a controlling idea?
☐ Do your similarities and differences support your topic sentence?
☐ Are your ideas in the correct order?
☐ Does your paragraph have a concluding sentence?

F. Edit Your Paragraph

Work with a partner or your teacher to edit your paragraph. Check spelling, punctuation, vocabulary, and grammar. Use the editing checklist below.

Editing Checklist

☐ Subject in every sentence?
☐ Verb in every sentence?
☐ Words in correct order?
☐ Sentences begin with a capital letter?
☐ Sentences end with a period directly at the end of a sentence?
☐ Sentences have a space between them?
☐ Commas in the correct place?
☐ Wrong words?
☐ Spelling?
☐ Missing words (use insertion mark: ^)?

G. Write Your Final Copy

When your rough draft has been edited, you can write the final copy of your paragraph.

Chapter

14 What's in a Name?

Pre-Reading

Discuss the answers to these questions with your classmates.

1. In early times, what do you think was the last name of each of these people?
2. What is your last name?
3. Is your last name made from two family names or one? Do you put your first name before or after your last name?
4. What do you think your last name means? Where do you think it came from?

Key Vocabulary

Do you know these words? Match the words with the meanings.

1. abbreviation ___d___   **a.** a special name for a product
2. characteristic ___e___   **b.** something that helps you recognize a place
3. honor ___f___   **c.** the first letter of a name
4. initial ___c___   **d.** short form
5. landmark ___b___   **e.** special qualities of someone or something
6. paperwork ___g___   **f.** show respect and admiration
7. trademark ___a___   **g.** the job of writing reports and records

Reading

What's in a Name?

Track 14

1   In the beginning, people didn't have last names or family names; they
just had a first name. We do not know when the custom of giving last names
started. Different areas and cultures started to use them at different times. But
even today, Icelanders, Tibetans, and Burmese do not use last names.

5   In English-speaking countries, most last names were connected to people's
occupations, personal **characteristics**, and where they lived. Many last
names are occupations. For example, John the *smith*, which means "one
who works with metal," became John Smith. Smith, by the way, is the most
common last name in the English-speaking world. Many other occupations,
10   such as cook, baker, carpenter, singer, and miller are last names too. This is
also true of German names. The name Müller, for example, is German for
miller, meaning "a person who crushes grain for bread." Other people took the
names of a place or a **landmark** near their homes. Roger, who lives near the
rivers, would become Roger Rivers. Other landmarks became last names such
15   as Woods, Hill, Stone, Field, and Lane. People's personal characteristics also
turned into names. Last names such as Small, Long, Strong, Moody, and Wild
all come from people's characteristics.

Many last names end in *son*. A long time ago, if a person's name was John
and his father's name was Albert, people would call him John, Albert's son.
20   As time passed, people shortened the name to John Albertson. Last names
of this type include Johnson, Peterson, Robertson, and Davidson. In Scotland
and Ireland, the word *Mac* or its **abbreviation** *Mc* is the word for *son*. For
example, the last name MacDonald would be the son of Donald.

In the West, it is the custom to put your family name last. But in some
25   Asian countries like China, Japan, Korea, and Vietnam, the family name
comes first, so your name is Smith John and not John Smith. In Spain and
Spanish-speaking countries, most people have two family names, although
in some situations they use only the first one. The first family name is the

father's family name, and the second family name is the mother's family
30   name. For example, in the name Marco Perez Martinez, Perez is the father's
name and Martinez is the mother's name.

    In English-speaking countries like Australia, Canada, England, and the
United States, as well as some countries like Vietnam in Southeast Asia,
many people have middle names. The reason for a middle name may be to
35   **honor** a relative. It may be the name of the grandfather or grandmother,
or one's parents may have liked this name for their child as well. Most
people abbreviate their middle name and just write the **initial**. Some people
like their middle name more than their first name. If this is the case, they
abbreviate their first name with an initial and use their middle name, or they
40   may not use their first name at all. For example, James Paul McCartney uses
his middle name and last name, Paul McCartney.

    People can, of course, change their names, but they have to complete
a lot of **paperwork**. There are some rules for this; for example, you can't
change your name to a famous person's name or a **trademark**. One man,
45   however—who was named Winfred Holley and had a white beard—changed
his name to Santa Claus. Another man from Hawaii had one of the longest
last names, Kikahiolanikonoikaouiaulani, and complained that he spent half
his life spelling his name. He did not change it, however.

Vocabulary

A. Vocabulary in Context

Complete these sentences with the following words.

3 abbreviation	4 initial	6 paperwork
1 characteristics	2 landmark	7 trademark
5 honor		

1. A long time ago, people named you after your personal _____.

2. A _____ such as a river, a hill, or a field were also last names.

3. Mr. is a/an _____ of Mister.

4. Some people don't write out all of their middle name. They just write the
_____.

5. Some middle names _____ a relative such as one's grandfather.

6. If you want to change your name, there is a lot of _____ to do.

7. You can't change your name to a _____.

Word Partnership	Use **honor** with:
n.	**code of** honor, **sense of** honor, honor **a ceasefire**
adj.	**great/highest** honor

B. Vocabulary in New Context

Answer the questions with complete sentences.

1. What are two of your personal characteristics?

_____

_____

2. What is the abbreviation of the word *abbreviation*?

The abbreviation of the word abbreviation is abb

_____

3. What is a landmark near where you live?

_____

_____

4. What are your initials?

_____

_____

5. To do what requires a lot of paperwork?

_____

_____

C. Vocabulary Building

Complete these sentences with the words from the box.

1	*2*	
to relate (*verb*)	**relative** (*noun*)	**related** (*adj.*)

1. I find it difficult _____ the two stories.
2. I have a _____ in California.

	3	*4*
to abbreviate (*verb*)	**abbreviation** (*noun*)	**abbreviated** (*adj.*)

3. The _____ for *doctor* is *Dr.*
4. *Miss* is an _____ form of the old word *mistress*.

6	*8*	*5*
to occupy (*verb*)	**occupation** (*noun*)	**occupied** (*adj.*)

5. I'm sorry. This seat is _____.
6. The new owners want _____ the house immediately.

Reading Comprehension

A. Looking for the Main Ideas

Circle the letter of the best answer.

1. In early times in English-speaking countries, last names _____.
   a. were not very common
   b. took the place of first names
   c. came from people's jobs and lives
   d. were mostly about people's characteristics

2. Customs of naming are _____.
   a. not the same, even within a country
   b. different around the world
   c. similar around the globe
   d. similar in Asian countries and Spanish-speaking countries

3. In places where there are middle names, people _____.
   a. always use their middle name to honor relatives
   b. usually use their middle name instead of their first name
   c. have parents who could not decide on a first name
   d. have different reasons and uses for their middle name

B. Looking for Details

Circle **T** if the sentence is true. Circle **F** if the sentence is false.

1. Today, Icelanders, Tibetans, and Koreans do not use last names.   **T**   **F**
2. Miller is the most common name in English-speaking countries.   **T**   **F**
3. In Scotland, the word *Mac* means *son*.   **T**   **F**
4. In Spanish-speaking countries, people put their family name first.   **T**   **F**
5. Most people use an initial for their middle name.   **T**   **F**
6. You cannot change your name to a famous person's name.   **T**   **F**

Discussion Questions

Discuss the answers to these questions with your classmates.

1. What are the most common last names in your country? What do they mean? Where did they come from?
2. Do you like your last name? Why or why not? If you could choose your last name, what would it be?
3. Do you have middle names in your country? Is there usually a reason for a middle name in your country, such as honoring a person? Do you have a middle name? If yes, why did your parents choose that name?

Critical Thinking Questions

Discuss the answers to these questions with your classmates.

1. Why do you think some first names make us think of certain characteristics, such as a weak, unattractive man, or an unattractive woman? What names make us think of these characteristics? What names seem to go with a strong, handsome man and a beautiful woman? What are some other names that make us think about certain characteristics in a person?
2. What first names were popular when you were a child? What first names are popular now? Why do you think popular names change with each generation?

Writing

Writing Model

Read the following business letter. It is a job application letter.

Model Letter

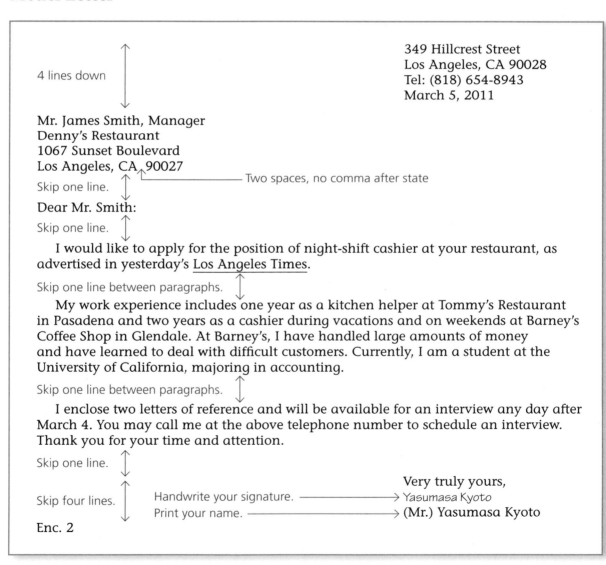

349 Hillcrest Street
Los Angeles, CA 90028
Tel: (818) 654-8943
March 5, 2011

4 lines down

Mr. James Smith, Manager
Denny's Restaurant
1067 Sunset Boulevard
Los Angeles, CA 90027

Skip one line. ———— Two spaces, no comma after state

Dear Mr. Smith:

Skip one line.

I would like to apply for the position of night-shift cashier at your restaurant, as advertised in yesterday's <u>Los Angeles Times</u>.

Skip one line between paragraphs.

My work experience includes one year as a kitchen helper at Tommy's Restaurant in Pasadena and two years as a cashier during vacations and on weekends at Barney's Coffee Shop in Glendale. At Barney's, I have handled large amounts of money and have learned to deal with difficult customers. Currently, I am a student at the University of California, majoring in accounting.

Skip one line between paragraphs.

I enclose two letters of reference and will be available for an interview any day after March 4. You may call me at the above telephone number to schedule an interview. Thank you for your time and attention.

Skip one line.

Skip four lines.

Very truly yours,

Handwrite your signature. ——→ *Yasumasa Kyoto*
Print your name. ——————→ (Mr.) Yasumasa Kyoto

Enc. 2

Writing Skills

A. Organizing: *Business Letter Form*

The writer's address and the date are in the upper right-hand corner of the page. Start the first word in each line at the same place on the line to form a block.

Notice the use of commas and periods. Do not use a comma before the ZIP code, which you write two spaces after the state postal abbreviation.

Abbreviations Used in Addresses

Apt.	=	Apartment	Ltd.	=	Limited
Ave.	=	Avenue	No.	=	Number
Blvd.	=	Boulevard	P.O.	=	Post Office
Co.	=	Company	Rd.	=	Road
Dept.	=	Department	St.	=	Street
Inc.	=	Incorporated			

The receiver's name and address are written on the left, starting four lines down from the date line. Again, start the first word in each line at the same place on the line to form a block.

The greeting is written one line down from the last line of the receiver's address. The standard greeting is **Dear (title + name)**. If you do not know the person's name, write **Dear Sir/Madam**. Put a colon (:) after the greeting.

Titles

Mr.	=	married or unmarried man
Ms.	=	married or unmarried woman
Mrs.	=	married woman
Miss	=	unmarried woman (no period after *Miss,* because it is not an abbreviation)

The *closing* goes two lines below the body of the letter. It should be in line with the beginning of the writer's address. Capitalize the first word of the closing, and place a comma after it.

Common Closings

Sincerely,

Sincerely yours,

Very truly yours,

Respectfully,

Cordially, (if you know the person you are writing to)

To sign your letter, first type or print your name four lines down from the closing. Your name should start at the same place as your closing. Next, handwrite your signature (in black or dark blue ink) between the closing and your typed name. Note that we write our first names first and family names last. Do not give your title unless your name may be unfamiliar to English speakers and the receiver may not know whether you are a man or woman. In this case, type your title in parentheses before your name.

If you are sending something with your letter, type the word **Enclosure** or its abbreviation, **Enc.**, at the left margin, below your name.

Address the envelope by writing your full name and complete address in the upper left-hand corner of the envelope. Write the receiver's name and address, as in the letter, in the middle of the envelope. Look at this example of an addressed envelope.

Yasumasa Kyoto
349 Hillcrest Street
Los Angeles, CA 90028

Stamp

Mr. James Smith, Manager
Denny's Restaurant
1067 Sunset Boulevard
Los Angeles, CA 90027

B. Business Letter Content

As a student, you may have to write a business letter to apply for a job or to a school. Or you may need to write a letter to ask for something, such as information about a program in a college. A business letter has three parts, just like a composition. Each part is usually one paragraph. However, in some cases the body may take more than one paragraph.

The following is an outline of a business letter:

Part 1: Introduction   State the purpose of your letter.

Part 2: Body   Give supporting information. (This may take more than one paragraph.)

Part 3: Conclusion   State what you will do or want the reader to do; say thank you.

Now look back at the model letter for a job application.

1. What is the purpose of the first paragraph?
2. What information does the second paragraph give? Is this information necessary?
3. Does the last paragraph ask for or announce an action and give thanks?

Exercise

Find the mistakes. There are 10 mistakes in punctuation and capitalization. Find and correct them.

As you know, you can address a woman as miss or mrs. If a woman is married, we address her as mrs. If she is not married, we address her as miss. However men do not have this Distinction. We address a man as mr if he is married or not. Now there is a new form of address for women. It is ms We can use this form if they are married or not.

Writing Practice

A. Write a Business Letter

Choose *one* of the four topics on the next page and write a short letter requesting the information given in parentheses. Address an envelope with both your name and address and the receiver's name and address. Pay attention to punctuation and capitalization.

1. ms. cheryl browne/director of admissions/university of texas/post office box 220/dallas/texas/75208 (Ask for an application form and information about the college. Ask for the TOEFL requirement.)
2. office of admission and records/glendale college/1500 north verdugo road/ glendale/ca/90028 (Ask that they send a copy of your transcripts to you. Give the semesters and years you attended.)
3. billing inquiries/national bank/post office box 31899/phoenix/az/85071 (Ask them to cancel your credit card. Give details.)
4. job application letter/lee's clothing supply store/246 summer street/boston/ ma/02115 (Apply for a job as a cashier.)

B. Write a Rough Draft

Write a rough draft of your letter using a word processing program.

C. Revise Your Rough Draft

Revise and edit your rough draft, using the business letter checklist below.

Business Letter Checklist

- [ ] Does your letter have the correct address?
- [ ] Does your letter have the correct date?
- [ ] Does your letter have an indent for each paragraph?
- [ ] Does your letter have the correct spacing between paragraphs?
- [ ] Does your letter have correct spelling, punctuation, and grammar?
- [ ] Does your letter have your signature and your printed name below it?

D. Write Your Final Copy

When your rough draft has been edited, you can write the final copy of your paragraph.

Weaving It Together

⏱ Timed Writing

Choose one of the following topics that you have not already written about in "Writing Practice." You have 50 minutes to write your paragraph.

1. Wedding customs in your country and in North America (or another country)
2. Past and present wedding customs (any country)
3. Wedding receptions for the wealthy and not so wealthy (any country)

Connecting to the Internet

A. Use the Internet to look up the following last names. Find out what country or culture each name is from and what it means.

Ainsworth Reyes Van Dyck
Gilbert Rousseau Wang
Rayner Schenck

B. Find out which is the most common name in the following countries: China, France, Japan, Korea, Mexico, United Kingdom, and United States.

What Do You Think Now?

Refer to page 161 at the beginning of this unit. Do you know the answers now? Complete the sentence, or circle the best answer.

1. Brides (wear/don't wear) white all over the world.
2. Many Chinese couples see a _____ for a suitable wedding day.
3. In the English-speaking world, _____ is the most common last name.
4. Many people in the U.S., England, and _____ have middle names.
5. In the U.S. you (can/cannot) change your name to a famous person's name.

What Do You Think?

Answer the questions with your best guess. Circle **Yes** or **No**.

Do you think . . .

1. all poems look the same?	**Yes**	**No**
2. there are poems with no punctuation marks?	**Yes**	**No**
3. a folktale is usually a funny story?	**Yes**	**No**
4. every culture has folktales?	**Yes**	**No**
5. folktales usually have a moral or lesson?	**Yes**	**No**

Chapter 15 Making Poetry of Plums

Pre-Reading

Discuss the answers to these questions with your classmates.

1. What fruit is in the picture?
2. If you were very hungry, would you eat it?
3. What is your favorite fruit? Why do you like it?

Key Vocabulary

Do you know these words? Match the words with the meanings.

1. icebox ___c___   **a.** stop being angry with someone; pardon someone
2. forgive ___a___   **b.** keep something for the future
3. delicious ___d___   **c.** refrigerator; a place to keep food cold
4. save ___b___   **d.** having a good taste

Reading

"This Is Just to Say"
by William Carlos Williams

This Is Just to Say

1   I have eaten
the plums
that were in
the **icebox**

5   and which
you were probably
saving
for breakfast

Forgive me
10   they were **delicious**
so sweet
and so cold

Vocabulary

A. Vocabulary in Context

Complete the sentences with the following words.

- delicious
- forgive
- icebox
- saving

1. We put the food in the _____ to keep it cold and fresh.
2. The plums tasted very good. They were _____.
3. I don't want to eat the plums now. I am _____ them for later.
4. I'm sorry that I upset you. Please _____ me.

B. Vocabulary in New Context

Answer these questions with complete sentences.

1. What fruit do you put in your icebox?

_____

_____

2. What is something you like to save?

_____

_____

3. What food do you think is delicious?

_____

_____

4. What is something you could never forgive?

_____

_____

C. Vocabulary Building

Complete these sentences with the words from the box.

to forgive (verb)	**forgiveness** (noun)	**forgiving** (adj.)

1. He asked for her _____ because he forgot her birthday.

2. She was not a _____ person.

to sweeten (verb)	**sweetness** (noun)	**sweet** (adj.)

3. She likes _____ her tea with honey.

4. Some tomatoes have a natural _____.

to ice (verb)	**ice** (noun)	**icy** (adj.)

5. It was difficult to drive because the road was _____.

6. Can I have some _____ in my water please?

Reading Comprehension

A. Understanding the Poem

Answer these questions with complete sentences.

1. Why did the writer write the poem?

_____

_____

2. What did the writer do that was wrong?

_____

_____

3. How does the writer feel about what he did?

_____

_____

4. Would you forgive the writer?

_____

_____

B. Recognizing Style

Work with a partner to answer the questions.

1. What tells you that this is a poem?

_____

_____

2. What do you notice about the writer's use of lines and of punctuation?

_____

_____

3. How is this poem different from a traditional poem?

_____

_____

4. What kind of patterns can you see in the poem?

_____

_____

5. Read the poem aloud. Mark the places where you pause. Compare your answers with those of your partner. Decide which reading sounds best to you.

Discussion Questions

Discuss the answers to these questions with your classmates.

1. Did you enjoy reading this poem? Why or why not?
2. Is it important to read poems? Why or why not?
3. Have you ever written poems? When and why?

Critical Thinking Questions

Discuss the answers to these questions with your classmates.

1. This poem is not about plums. It is about the person who takes the plums. What does the poem tell us about that person?
2. Which words in the poem help us to see and taste the plums? If you had to write a poem, what subject would you choose and why? What pictures and feelings would you try to create in the reader's mind?

Writing

Writing Skills

Turning a Dialogue into a Poem

Imagine that the poem was spoken as a conversation, instead of a poem. It might sound like this:

A: Who ate the plums that were in the icebox?

B: I did. I'm sorry.

A: I was saving them for breakfast. Why did you eat them?

B: They looked so sweet and so cold. They were delicious.

Read the following dialogues. Choose one that you like. Work with a partner. Try replacing some of the key words in the poem with words from the dialogue to make a new poem.

Dialogue 1

A: Who cut the rose from the rosebush that was in my garden?

B: I did. I'm sorry.

A: I waited so long for it to flower. I wanted to wear it to the dance on Saturday. Why did you do that?

B: It was so beautiful and had such a sweet smell. I wanted to have it.

Dialogue 2

A: Who crashed my new car, which was parked in my driveway? It was like my baby.

B: I did. I'm sorry.

A: I was going to drive it to work today. Why did you take it?

B: I wanted my friends to think it was mine.

Writing Practice

Write your own version of the poem using a different topic.

Chapter

16 Stone Soup: A Folktale

Pre-Reading

Discuss the answers to these questions with your classmates.

1. What are some famous folktales?
2. Why do people like them?
3. What is your favorite folktale?

Key Vocabulary

Do you know these words? Match the words with the meanings.

1. famine _____
2. tent _____
3. glance _____
4. steam _____
5. curiosity _____
6. rumor _____

a. look at something briefly
b. desire to find out more about something
c. news that may or may not be true
d. a time when many people have no food
e. temporary shelter that a person can carry
f. what rises into the air when water gets very hot

Reading

Stone Soup

Track 16

1   **T**his story happened a long time ago, somewhere in Europe, in the middle
of a bitter winter. There was a terrible **famine** throughout the land. In the
A   villages, people were so hungry that each family kept their food hidden away,
so that no one else would be able to find it. They hardly spoke to each other,
5   and if any food was found, they fought over it.

One day, a poor traveler arrived in a village and set up his **tent** by the side
B   of the road. He had with him a large pot, a wooden spoon, and a stone.

"You can't stay here," said the villagers. "There's no food for you!" And
they raced back to their houses to make sure no one stole their food while
10   they were away.

"That doesn't matter," said the stranger. "I have everything I need."

He gathered sticks and built a fire in the middle of the main square. Then
he placed his pot on the fire and added some water. He **glanced** around
and noticed that he was being watched from every window and from every
15   doorway. He smiled with satisfaction as the **steam** rose from the pot. Next, he
took an ordinary stone from his pocket, which he carefully placed in the pot.
He stirred the soup and waited patiently for it to boil.

C   By this time, the villagers were full of **curiosity**. Several of them had
gathered around the pot. "What are you making?" they asked.

20   "Stone soup," replied the man. "It smells good, doesn't it?" And he sniffed
the soup and smiled in anticipation. "Of course, a little salt and pepper would
really help the flavor."

"I think I could find some salt and pepper," said one of the women, and
she ran back to her house to fetch the salt and pepper to add to the soup.

25   "How tasty it would be with a tiny piece of garlic," said the traveler.

"I might have a tiny piece of garlic," said another villager.

"If only we had some potatoes, too, then it would really be delicious," said
the stranger.

"I'll get you a potato," said another man and rushed home to fetch it.

30   Soon the **rumor** had spread around the whole village. Someone was making a delicious soup with a special stone. People came from every house

D   to smell the bubbling soup, and each of them brought an extra ingredient to make the soup taste even better. They were so hungry, and the soup smelled so good. "It must be that special stone," they said.

35   Finally, the man declared that the soup was ready and it was time to eat. The villagers each brought a dish, and there was plenty of food for everyone. They talked and laughed, and for a while they forgot the famine and the cold. Even long after the famine had ended, people still remembered that night and the finest soup they had ever tasted.

Vocabulary

A. Vocabulary in Context

Complete these sentences with the following words.

famine	glanced	steam
curiosity	rumor	tent

1. A _____ is a shelter that you can fold up and carry with you.

2. The news may be true, or it may just be a _____.

3. When there is no food in a country, there is a _____.

4. They asked a lot of questions because they could not control their _____.

5. He _____ at the book, but he didn't look at it carefully.

6. When you boil water, you can see _____.

Word Partnership	Use **steam** with:
n.	steam **bath, clouds of** steam, steam **engine,** steam **pipes,** steam **turbine**
adj.	steam **powered, rising** steam

B. Vocabulary in New Context

Answer the questions with complete sentences.

1. What can we do to prevent famines?

_____

2. What kinds of rumors do you sometimes hear or see in the news?

_____

3. Have you ever stayed in a tent? When? Where?

_____

4. When you buy vegetables, do you just glance at them or do you look at them carefully?

_____

5. What kinds of things make you curious?

_____

6. What can steam be used for?

_____

C. Vocabulary Building

Complete these sentences with the words from the box.

to anticipate (*verb*)	**anticipation** (*noun*)	**anticipated** (*adj.*)

1. This is the most _____ show of the year.
2. He answered in _____ of my question.

to satisfy (*verb*)	**satisfaction** (*noun*)	**satisfied** (*adj.*)

3. I wasn't _____ with the results of the test.
4. He gets _____ out of helping people.

| to steam (*verb*) | steam (*noun*) | steamed (*adj.*) |

5. She likes _____ all of her vegetables.

6. You can see the _____ when the water boils.

Reading Comprehension

A. Understanding the Story

Answer the questions with complete sentences.

1. What was happening in the villages of the land?

_____

2. Why were the villagers hiding their food?

_____

3. Why were they unfriendly to the traveler?

_____

4. Why were they curious about the stone soup?

_____

5. What kind of man was the traveler?

_____

6. How did he make the villagers share their food?

_____

7. What was the traveler's trick?

_____

8. Why would the villagers never forget the stone soup?

_____

B. Interpreting the Story

Circle the letter of the best answer.

1. In the story, the villagers represent _____.
  a. people who like to cook
  b. people who work together
  c. people who are generous
  d. people who think only of themselves

2. In the story, the traveler represents _____.
  a. someone who helps people to work in a team
  b. someone who forces people to like each other
  c. someone who gives help when it is needed
  d. someone who prefers to be alone

3. In the story, the soup represents _____.
  a. something everyone wants but can't have
  b. something everyone can make individually
  c. something everyone can make together
  d. something everyone hates

4. What is the moral (the lesson) of the story?
  a. Everyone can be successful if he or she wants.
  b. No one is better than anyone else.
  c. People can achieve more by helping each other.
  d. Think before you act.

C. Recognizing Style

Work with a partner to answer the questions.

1. What tells you that this is a folktale?

_____

2. Are the characters in the story realistic? Why or why not?

_____

3. The story has four parts, labeled *A*, *B*, *C*, and *D*. Match each part with one of the descriptions below. Which part describes each of the following?

_____ Mysterious events that make the reader curious
_____ The setting for the story
_____ A happy conclusion to the story
_____ The meaning of the mysterious events

4. Does the story use a direct or indirect method of presenting its main meaning? Do you think this is effective? Why or why not?

Discussion Questions

Discuss the answers to these questions with your classmates.

1. How did you learn about folktales in your culture?
2. Do you think that folktales are important? How important are they, and why?
3. Are folktales less important today than they were in the past? Why?
4. What can we learn from folktales, and how useful are they in our daily lives?

Critical Thinking Questions

Discuss the answers to these questions with your classmates.

1. What is the lesson in this folktale?
2. Children must learn some important lessons about life and about living in society. What are some of these lessons? Do you know any folktales that teach these lessons?

Creating a Modern-Day Folktale

Work with a partner. Think of a situation where people have to work together to create something. Make a list of three or four such situations. Now retell the story of stone soup in a modern setting, using one of these situations.

Exercise

Find the mistakes. There are 10 mistakes in grammar, punctuation, capitalization, and spelling. Find and correct them.

The old Queen wanted to find out whether the girl was a real Princess. So she goes to the bedrom took all the bedding off the bed and put a pea on the bottom. Then, she took 20 mattresses and put it on top of pea. Finally she put 20 feather beds on top of the mattresses.

Writing Practice

Using Adjectives in Stories

1. Read the story again, and underline all the adjectives—for example, *in the middle of a bitter winter*. Notice how these words help to create a vivid picture.

2. Work in pairs. Read the paragraph below. What kinds of adjectives can you add to make the story more interesting? Add as many adjectives as you can, and rewrite the paragraph. Read your version to the rest of the class.

   A long time ago, in a <u>distant</u> country, a **1.** _____ girl lived with her **2.** _____ stepmother and two **3.** _____ stepsisters. Her **4.** _____ mother was dead, and her **5.** _____ father had married again. The **6.** _____ wife and her two **7.** _____ daughters hated the **8.** _____ stepdaughter

and forced her to wear **9.** _____ clothes and do all kinds of
10. _____ work around the **11.** _____ house. One
day, a **12.** _____ letter arrived in the mail. . . .

3. How does the story continue? Write your own ending.

4. Think of folktales you know. Write the first line and the last line. See if your
group can guess the story.

Weaving It Together

⏱ Timed Writing

Choose a folktale you know from "Writing Practice," question 4. You have 50 minutes to write your folktale in the form of a paragraph.

Connecting to the Internet

A. Look up poems on the Internet. Find one poem about each of the following themes: love, nature, youth, and old age. Which poem was your favorite, and why? Share this poem with your classmates.

B. Use the Internet to find a folktale from your country. Did you know the folktale before you found it online? If so, are there any differences between the way you remember the story and the way it is told on the Internet? Tell the story to your classmates, and explain the lesson it teaches.

What Do You Think Now?

Refer to page 187 at the beginning of this unit. Do you know the answers now? Complete the sentence, or circle the best answer.

1. All poems (look/don't look) the same.
2. There are poems with no _____ marks.
3. A folktale (is/isn't) usually a funny story.
4. Every culture has _____.
5. Folktales usually (have/don't have) a moral or lesson.

Expanding a Paragraph into an Essay

Sample Student Paragraph

<table>
<tr><td>○</td><td></td></tr>
<tr><td></td><td>Learning a Foreign Language</td></tr>
<tr><td>Topic sentence becomes thesis statement.</td><td>There are a lot of processes to go through in order to learn</td></tr>
<tr><td>Support Sentence 1</td><td>a foreign language. First, you have to like the people who speak</td></tr>
<tr><td>Support Sentence 2</td><td>that language. Then you have to find either a tutor or a teacher</td></tr>
<tr><td>Support Sentence 3</td><td>to help you with the language. After finding a person to teach</td></tr>
<tr><td></td><td>you that language, you must work hard to understand what he</td></tr>
<tr><td>○
Conclusion sentence</td><td>or she is teaching you. In conclusion, I think learning a foreign</td></tr>
<tr><td></td><td>language is very useful and a lot of fun.</td></tr>
</table>

Sample Student Essay

○	
	Learning a Foreign Language
Introduction	Learning a foreign language can be fun and interesting. You can hear and understand what people from other countries are saying. It feels good knowing what others are talking about. It is
Thesis statement	not easy learning a different language. There are a lot of processes to go through in order to learn a foreign language.
Body Paragraph 1	First you have to like the people who speak that language. You have to know the culture and the people. It makes learning less complicated. For example, I really like French music, and I want to understand the words of the songs. Then you have a
○	reason to start learning the language.
Body Paragraph 2	Then you have to find either a tutor or a teacher to help you with the language. You can do that by contacting some schools or asking your advisor. Having friends who speak that language can be very nice, too. They can help you to know that language out of class. For example, I can go to a French movie with a French friend and then talk about it.
Body Paragraph 3	After finding a person to teach you that language, you must work hard to understand what he or she is teaching you. Make sure you ask questions if you have any problems. When you are comfortable talking and writing that language is when I think you have accomplished your goal.
Conclusion	In conclusion, I think learning a foreign language is very useful and a lot of fun. It helps you a lot in finding a job. It makes you feel smart knowing what others might not know. Learning a
○	language can be fascinating and thrilling. Who knows what you can do with that language!

Photo Credits

This page constitutes an extension of the copyright page. We have made every effort to trace the ownership of all copyrighted material and to secure permission from copyright holders. In the event of any question arising as to the use of any material, we will be pleased to make the necessary corrections in future printings. Thanks are due to the following authors, publishers, and agents for permission to use the material indicated.

Chapter 1. 1: left, © AP Images/Chris Pizzello; center, © Alinari Archives/CORBIS; right, © AP Images/Evan Agostini; **2:** left, © Ariel Skelley/CORBIS; right, © Corbis/SuperStock

Chapter 2. 15: © Jose Luis Pelaez, Inc./CORBIS

Chapter 3. 27: © Fukuhara, Inc./CORBIS **28:** left, © John Smith RF/Corbis; center right, © Zoltán Novák/Shutterstock; bottom, © Danny E Hooks/Shutterstock;

Chapter 4. 41: © Jonathan Kingston/Aurora Photos/Corbis

Chapter 5. 55: © Matthieu Ricard/Getty Images **56:** © Philippe Body/Hemis/Corbis

Chapter 6. 67: © Image Source RF/Getty Images

Chapter 7. 81: left, © AP Images/Vincent Yu; center, © AP Images/Alex Brandon; right, © AP Images/Ted S. Warren; **82:** © Will & Deni McIntyre/Getty Images

Chapter 8. 94: © CORBIS

Chapter 9. 107: © AP Images/Mike Meadows **108:** © Jim Reed/Science Faction/Corbis

Chapter 10. 121: © Gary Bell/Corbis

Chapter 11. 133: © Jean-Christophe Bott/epa/Corbis **134:** © AP Images/Paul Sakuma

Chapter 12. 146: left, © Robography/Alamy; center left, © Lauren Burke/Getty Images; center right, © Ruth Boraggina; Michigan; bottom right, © Juniors Bildarchiv/Alamy

Chapter 13. 161: © thefinalmiracle/Shutterstock **162:** © iofoto/Shutterstock

Chapter 14. 175: left, © Bambu Productions/Getty Images; center left, © Ulrik Tofte RF/Getty Images; center right, © Per Magnus Persson/Getty Images; right, © Jeremy Liebman/Getty Images

Chapter 15. 187: © Yellowj/Shutterstock **188:** © Corrado Poli RF/Getty Images

Chapter 16. 195: © Studio Eye/Corbis

Skills Index

Grammar and Usage

Clauses
    Dependent clauses, 74–75
    Main clauses, 74–75
Comma, 116
Conjunctions
    Coordinating conjunctions, 21–24
however, 169–170
Nouns
    Proper nouns, 10
Pronouns, 10
so and *therefore*, 141–143
Time and place expressions, 116

Listening/Speaking

Discussion, 2, 7, 15, 20, 28, 34, 41, 46, 56, 61, 67, 72, 82, 88, 94, 98, 99, 108, 114, 121, 126, 134, 139, 146, 151, 162, 167, 175, 180, 190, 194, 196, 202
Listening to selections, 3–4, 16–17, 29–30, 42–43, 57–58, 68–69, 83–84, 95–96, 109–110, 122–123, 135–136, 147–148, 163–164, 176–177, 191, 197–198
Pre-reading activities, 2, 15, 28, 41, 56, 67, 82, 94, 108, 121, 134, 146, 162, 175, 190, 196

Reading

Comprehension
    Details, 7, 19–20, 33, 46, 61, 71–72, 87, 98, 113, 125–126, 139, 150, 167, 180
    Main ideas, 6, 19, 32, 45, 60–61, 71, 86, 97–98, 112, 125, 138, 150, 166, 179
Informational text, 3–4, 16–17, 29–30, 42–43, 57–58, 68–69, 83–84, 95–96, 109–110, 122–123, 135–136, 147–148, 163–164, 176–177, 191, 197–198
Literary forms
    Folktale, 196–205
Informational text, 16–17, 29–30, 42–43, 57–58, 68–69, 83–84, 95–96, 109–110, 122–123, 135–136, 147–148, 163–164, 176–177, 191, 197–198
Poetry, 193
Recognizing style, 201–202
Pre-reading, 2, 15, 28, 41, 56, 67, 82, 94, 108, 121, 134, 146, 162, 175, 190, 196
Recognizing style, 193–194, 201–202

Technology—Internet

Apple/Microsoft, 159
Biotechnology, 159
Birthday celebrations, 79
Blind people, 106
Delicacies, 53
Festivals/holidays, 79
Food, 53
Left-handed people, 26
Names and culture, 186
Natural disasters, 132
Phrenology, 26

Test-taking Skills

Circle best answer, 6, 19, 26, 32, 36, 37, 45, 48–49, 60–61, 71, 86, 97–98, 106, 112, 125, 132, 138, 150, 166–167, 179, 186, 201
Critical thinking questions, 7, 20, 34, 46, 61, 72, 88, 98, 114, 126, 139, 151, 167, 180, 194, 202
Discussion questions, 2, 7, 15, 20, 28, 34, 41, 46, 56, 61, 67, 72, 82, 88, 94, 98, 99, 108, 114, 121, 126, 134, 139, 146, 151, 162, 167, 175, 180, 190, 194, 196, 202
Fill in blank, 18–19, 32, 43, 45, 58–60, 69–70, 84, 86, 96–97, 112, 123–125, 136–138, 149, 164–166, 177–179, 191, 192, 198–200
Matching, 2, 15, 28, 41, 56, 67, 82, 94, 108, 121, 134, 146, 162, 175, 190, 196, 202

Sentence completion, 4–6, 17–19, 26, 30–33, 44, 53, 58–61, 70–72, 84–85, 87, 97, 106, 110–113, 123–126, 132, 136–139, 148–149, 159, 164–166, 177–179, 186, 191–194, 198–202

True-or-false questions, 7, 19–20, 46, 98, 150, 167, 180

Yes or no questions, 1, 27, 55, 107, 133, 161, 189

Topics

Celebrations and special days, 55–80
    Celebrating fifteen, 67–80
    Tihar: Festival of Lights, 55–66
Customs and traditions, 161–186
    Weddings, 161–174
    What's in a name, 175–186
Famous people, 81–106
    Louis Braille, 81–93
    World's most unusual millionaire, 94–106
Food, 27–53
    Delicacies, 41–53
    Potatoes, 27–40
Inventions, 133–159
    Biotechnology, 146–159
    Yahoo!, 133–145
Nature's disasters, 107–132
    Killer bees, 121–132
    Lightning, 107–120
Personality, 1–26
    Right brain/left brain, 1–14
    Shape of face, 15–26
Readings from literature, 189–205
    Folktales, 196–205
    Poetry, 189–195

Vocabulary

Building, 6, 18–19, 32, 45, 60, 70–71, 86, 97, 112, 124–125, 138, 149, 166, 179, 192, 199–200
In context, 4, 5, 17–18, 30–31, 43–44, 58–59, 69–70, 84–86, 96–97, 110–111, 123–124, 136–137, 148–149, 164–165, 177–178, 191–192, 198–199
Key, 2, 15, 28, 41, 56, 67, 82, 94, 108, 134, 146, 162, 175, 190, 196

Writing

Adjectives in stories, 203–204
Business letter form, 182
Capitalization, 9–12
Dialogue into poem, 195
Exercises, 10–13, 23–24, 36–37, 48–50, 63, 74–76, 101–103, 115–117, 128–129, 142–143, 154–156, 170–171, 203
Finding and correcting mistakes, 11, 25, 38, 50, 64, 76, 91, 103, 117, 129, 143, 156, 172, 184
Folktales, 203–204
Left/right brain, 14
Organizing
    Advantages and disadvantages, 152–154
    Business letter form, 182–185
    Cause-and-effect paragraph, 140–141
    Common closings, 183
    Comparing and contrasting, 168–169
    Compound sentences, 21–24
    Dependent clauses, 74–75
    Describing processes, 62–63, 73–74
    Examples, 100–102
    Fact or opinion, 154–155
    Giving reasons, 127–129
    Narrative paragraph, 115–117
    Showing addition, 154–155
    Time order wording, 115–116
    Transitions, 154–155, 169–172
    Unity, 89
Paragraphs, 8–9, 25, 38–40, 50–52, 64–66, 76–78, 91–93, 103–105, 117–120, 129–131, 143–145, 156–158, 172–174
Punctuation, 9–10, 13, 63–64, 75, 116–117
Sentences
    Compound, 8–9, 21–24
    Concluding, 49–50
    Irrelevant, 90–91
    Joining, 21–22
    Supporting, 47–49
    Topic, 35–38
Timed writing, 26, 53, 79, 106, 132, 159, 186
Titles, 12–13
Writing model, 35, 47, 62, 73, 89, 100, 115, 127, 140, 152, 168, 181